DOUBLE OR NOTHING?

DOUBLE OR

PUBLISHED BY UNIVERSITY PRESS OF NEW ENGLAND

HANOVER AND LONDON

NOTHING?

Jewish Families and Mixed Marriage

Sylvia Barack Fishman

BRANDEIS UNIVERSITY PRESS

Brandeis University Press

Published by University Press of New England,

37 Lafayette St., Lebanon, NH 03766

© 2004 by Brandeis University Press

All rights reserved

Printed in the United States of America

5 4 3 2 1

Library of Congress Cataloging-in-Publication Data

Fishman, Sylvia Barack, 1942–

Double or nothing? : Jewish familes and mixed marriage / Sylvia
Barack Fishman.

  p.   cm.—(Brandeis series in American Jewish history, culture, and life)
(Brandeis series on Jewish Women)

Includes bibliographical references and index.

ISBN 1–58465–206–3 (cloth : alk. paper)

1. Interfaith marriage—United States.   2. Jews—United States—Social
conditions.   3. Jewish families—United States.   I. Title.   II. Series.
III. Series: Brandeis series on Jewish women

HQ1031.F56 2004

306.84′3′0973—dc22   2003021956

BRANDEIS SERIES IN AMERICAN
JEWISH HISTORY, CULTURE, AND LIFE

Jonathan D. Sarna, Editor
Sylvia Barack Fishman, Associate Editor

Jack Wertheimer, 1997
A People Divided: Judaism in Contemporary America

Beth S. Wenger and Jeffrey Shandler, editors, 1998
Encounters with the "Holy Land": Place, Past and Future in American Jewish Culture

David Kaufman, 1998
Shul with a Pool: The "Synagogue-Center" in American Jewish History

Roberta Rosenberg Farber and Chaim I. Waxman, editors, 1999
Jews in America: A Contemporary Reader

Murray Friedman and Albert D. Chernin, editors, 1999
A Second Exodus: The American Movement to Free Soviet Jews

Stephen J. Whitfield, 1999
In Search of American Jewish Culture

Naomi W. Cohen, 1999
Jacob H. Schiff: A Study in American Jewish Leadership

Barbara Kessel, 2000
Suddenly Jewish: Jews Raised as Gentiles

Jonathan N. Barron and Eric Murphy Selinger, editors, 2000
Jewish American Poetry: Poems, Commentary, and Reflections

Steven T. Rosenthal, 2001
Irreconcilable Differences: The Waning of the American Jewish Love Affair with Israel

Pamela S. Nadell and Jonathan D. Sarna, editors, 2001
Women and American Judaism: Historical Perspectives

Annelise Orleck, with photographs by Elizabeth Cooke, 2001
The Soviet Jewish Americans

Ilana Abramovitch and Seán Galvin, editors, 2001
Jews of Brooklyn

Ranen Omer-Sherman, 2002
Diaspora and Zionism in American Jewish Literature: Lazarus, Syrkin, Reznikoff, and Roth

BRANDEIS SERIES ON JEWISH WOMEN

Shulamit Reinharz, General Editor
Joyce Antler, Associate Editor
Sylvia Barack Fishman, Associate Editor

The Brandeis Series on Jewish Women is an innovative book series created by The Hadassah-Brandeis Institute. BSJW publishes a wide range of books by and about Jewish women in diverse contexts and time periods, of interest to scholars and the educated public. The series fills a major gap in Jewish learning by focusing on the lives of Jewish women and Jewish gender studies.

Kalpana Misra and Melanie S. Rich, *Jewish Feminism in Israel: Some Contemporary Perspectives,* 2003

Farideh Goldin, *Wedding Song: Memoirs of an Iranian Jewish Woman,* 2003

Rochelle L. Millen, *"A Time to Be Born, a Time to Die": Women, Birth, and Death in Jewish Law and Practice,* 2003

Sylvia Barack Fishman, *Double or Nothing? Jewish Families and Mixed Marriage,* 2004

Iris Parush, *Women's Reading and the Eastern European Jewish Enlightenment,* 2004

Tamar Ross, *Expanding the Palace of Torah: Orthodoxy and Feminism,* 2004

For Phil
With love
Twice Chai

Contents

Acknowledgments

It is my pleasure to thank the individuals and institutions who contributed to the research and writing of this book. I owe a great debt of gratitude to many Brandeis University friends, especially Len Saxe and the Cohen Center for Modern Jewish Studies; Len's wisdom was invaluable in the planning and implementation of my original research, and in comments on this manuscript. As always, I am grateful to Jonathan Sarna in his role as series editor and for his many helpful comments, and to chair Marc Brettler and the faculty and staff of the Near Eastern and Judaic Studies Department. My work has been supported and encouraged in many ways by founding director Shulamit Reinharz and the Hadassah-Brandeis Institute, board chairs Diane Troderman and Annie Sandler, and colleagues Helene Greenberg, Nancy Vineberg, and Debby Olins. Not least, Brandeis University Press editor Phyllis Deutsch provided a keen literary eye as well as patience and support, and the UPNE staff were splendid.

Double or Nothing? Jewish Families and Mixed Marriage draws on original interview research that was supported by David Singer and Steven Bayme at the American Jewish Committee, and it would not have been possible without them. David read portions of this manuscript as well and made insightful comments. A hearty thank you to the couples in New England, New Jersey, Atlanta, and Denver who opened their homes and hearts to me and my exceptional team, including Naomi Bar Yam, project manager, and interviewers Christian J. Churchill, Lila Corwin, Margie Nesson, Rachel Rockenmacher, and Mark Rosen. I would also like to thank the Dovetail Institute for inviting me to address their August 2002 conference in Chicago, providing the opportunity to hear additional ideas and experiences of dual-faith families.

Ben Phillips brilliantly deciphered the 2000 NJPS to produce useful statistical tables. My assistants Sarah Slone and Suzy Klein accomplished numerous tasks with skill, speed, patience, and good humor during the process of revising this manuscript. Help in gathering materials on cultural contexts was provided by HBI student interns Dena Wigder and Aviva Dautch. Anne Lawrence and Jennifer Coveney in the NEJS office were always gracious and helpful. Nancy Zibman competently created the index.

Colleagues across the country made useful suggestions and shared their own research with me as I wrote this book. I would especially like to thank Bruce Phillips, Charles Kadushin, and Dru Greenwood for encouraging me to look at my data in new ways, and Bonnie Cousens for providing information about secular Jewish humanism.

Writing a book that analyzes people's marital choices and negotiations is a compelling enterprise, often drawing on a great deal of psychic as well as intellectual and organizational energy. My love and gratitude go to the man who helps me, again and again, through the ups and downs of this writing life, my husband, Phil.

DOUBLE OR NOTHING?

INTRODUCTION: FOLLOWING OUR HEARTS

America's promises are dramatically symbolized and fulfilled by marriage across boundaries, according to some observers. Americans following their own hearts, unfettered by familial and communal preferences, illustrate the triumph of Romantic values such as the sanctity of the individual and the sacredness of personal passions. Line-crossing weddings are "the supreme expression of the contemporary ideal of marriage as a grand, individualistic romance detached from society's strictures—the ideal to which contemporary Americans are wedded, for better or for worse," as Rebecca Mead recently suggested in the *New Yorker.* Mead argues that the policies of the *New York Times* wedding announcements section are symbolic of a profound attitudinal change toward the meaning of marriage:

> The wedding announcement as love story is of a piece with the popular understanding that marriage is primarily a romance rather than, as has historically been the case, a pragmatic contractual arrangement sanctioned by a larger community. This is no surprise, since those earlier characteristics of marriage have been largely stripped away. . . . Wedding announcements are now not so much accounts of upheld tradition as celebrations of individualism.[1]

Looking at marriages across religious and ethnic lines, religious bigotries and ethnic hatreds seem conquered when Americans whose grandparents were Orthodox Greeks, Irish or Italian Catholics, English Episcopalians, German Lutherans, Chinese Buddhists, or Lithuanian Jews walk down the aisle, gazing at each other with love. The proliferation of mixed marriages also seems to diminish xenophobia when family members from diverse cultural backgrounds learn to understand and care about each other. As one member of an interfaith marriage said recently, "We are making the world a better place just by raising our children to participate in two religions."[2]

More Americans marry across ethnic and religious lines because boundaries have become so permeable—and boundaries become ever more permeable as more Americans create interethnic and interfaith homes.

This book follows Jews and non-Jews as they step through the looking glass into a world familiar yet different. Some of these couples decide to raise their children in one religion, Jewish or Christian, others to raise them in both religions, still others with no formal religion in the household.

The religious character of mixed-married households is seldom the result of one definitive unilateral decision. Husbands and wives usually negotiate over a long period of time with each other—and with themselves! To an extent seldom realized, mixed-marrying Americans often construct a more pointed definition of their own ethnoreligious identity, as well as a new understanding of the identities of their spouses. A number of Jewish mixed-married spouses commented, "I never felt so Jewish until I married my Christian husband/wife." Faced with a newly poignant awareness of self and other, mixed-married couples are challenged to create a mix that works for them. This challenge is heightened as they give birth to and raise children, interact with extended family, and make connections with Jewish and/or Christian religious and communal institutions.

Drawing on original interviews with mixed-married men and women, focus group discussions with their teenage children, materials produced by communal, secular, and religious organizations, and conferences, books, and films created by and for interfaith audiences, this book examines family dynamics in mixed-married households.[3] Today's interfaith families are placed within their American contexts, including their depiction in literature, film, and popular culture, and considered against the backdrop of historical Jewish societies. Economic, cultural, and socioreligious outcomes of mixed marriage are explored. The book concludes by discussing the implications of these phenomena for those concerned with the transmission of the Jewish cultural heritage and the future of American Jewish life.

America Is Different

While some communal leaders speak of mixed marriage as though it were a simple "symptom" of assimilation, mixed marriage in America today is different from most historical patterns because the situation of Jews today departs significantly from past eras. If Jews from most places and periods of Jewish history were transported via time machine into twenty-first-century America, they would be astonished by the unprecedented acceptance enjoyed by contemporary Jews.

Twenty-first-century America fulfills in many ways the freedoms Emancipation promised but did not deliver. Following centuries of intermittent and sometimes sustained persecution, Western Europe's Jews were first offered the opportunity to become educated citizens of their host countries during the eighteenth century—but only if they abandoned their distinctive Jewish lifestyles. Apostasy—conversion to Christianity—often continued to seem to represent the only ticket to full participation. Throughout the eighteenth, nineteenth, and the first decades of the twentieth centuries, significant numbers of Jews bought that ticket and traveled away from Jewish peoplehood, becoming fiercely nationalistic patriots of their adopted lands. East European Jews, gradually and more incompletely emancipated during the nineteenth and twentieth centuries, believed it was unlikely they would receive full equality as distinctively practicing Jews in their European homelands. While millions emigrated to America and thousands became Jewish nationalists supporting the Zionist cause, many of those who remained in Russia and Eastern Europe embraced total secularism and communist movements that promised them a classless society, putatively free of religious and racial hatreds.

By the middle of the twentieth century, these dreams of acceptance and the eradication of antisemitic prejudice through the abandonment of Jewish mores had repeatedly proved bitterly delusionary. European Jewish populations and culture were eviscerated during the Holocaust. Stalin and other communist leaders rejected religion but not religious prejudice, persecuting, imprisoning, and killing Jews with particular venom. Most Jewish communities in Arab and Moslem countries were decimated in the decades following the establishment of the State of Israel, sending their Jewish populations fleeing to Israel, the Americas, and elsewhere.

Today, Jews comprise a tiny minority worldwide and in all countries except for Israel: internationally, well over one billion Muslims and two billion

Christians can be compared to thirteen million Jews. In the United States, Jews are less than 2.5 percent of the population; Christians are 84 percent. America and Israel have emerged as home to the world's two most numerous Jewish populations: at the turn of the twenty-first century, 43 percent of the world's Jews (approximately six million) lived in the United States and 37 percent (nearly five million) lived in Israel.[4]

The condition of American Jews today is in many ways idyllic. America is home not only to the world's largest but arguably its freest Jewish community: during the nineteenth and especially the twentieth centuries, despite cycles of antisemitism notably weaker than the widespread virulence of European models, Jews as a group became one of the most highly educated American populations, climbing socioeconomic ladders and gaining reputations as exemplars of the American success story. In the years after World War II, concerted American sociopolitical efforts helped to diminish antisemitism and other bigotries. The social upheavals of the late 1960s and early 1970s further eroded white Christian cultural hegemony and validated the legitimacy of diverse ethnic traditions. Boundaries between American Jews and non-Jews have now become so permeable as to be virtually nonexistent, and Jews are welcome in nearly every school, business, or neighborhood.

Even more extraordinary than the opportunities accorded American Jews is the fact that they currently enjoy these blessings without needing to submerge their ethnic and religious particularism. Within the current multicultural American milieu, Jews—like other ethnic groups—are encouraged to celebrate their differences. In this tolerant environment, ethnic cultures have undergone an extraordinary revitalization. A substantial proportion of American Jews has become newly engaged by Jewish culture, history, and religious expression. Jews today can feel both more Jewish and more American by exploring their distinctiveness. Many have called this upsurge of interest in and opportunities for creating dialogue with historical Judaism a "renaissance." At the same time that Jewish leaders celebrate this renaissance, however, they are concerned about assimilation and high rates of intermarriage.

Discussing Ethnicity and Mixed Marriage

No social phenomenon expresses the extraordinary new status of American Jews more than their attractiveness as romantic and marital partners for mainstream Christian Americans. The permeable boundaries that allow Americans to enjoy manifestations of each other's ethnic heritage have increased rates of marriage across ethnic and religious lines. Many, perhaps most, Americans applaud the decreased intolerance that allows men and women from differing ethnic and religious heritages to befriend and marry each other. Indeed, some scholars feel that such mixed marriages are not only the result of decreased bigotry but also one of the major causes of increased tolerance. More than one observer has speculated that the equanimity greeting the 1998 vice-presidential candidacy of Senator Joseph Lieberman was positively influenced by the widespread presence of Jews in many American Christian families.

If intermarriage, as some observers claim, is a blessing, American Jews are certainly among the prime beneficiaries. Recent statistical studies show that about half of all recent marriages involving a Jew have been marriages to non-Jews. Unlike the much smaller number of Jewish mixed marriages at mid-century, Jews who marry non-Jews today do not necessarily have an agenda of escaping the Jewish community. Many of them are interested in maintaining at least some ties with their own ethnoreligious heritage. On the other hand, unlike mixed marriages at mid-century, which were primarily marriages of Jewish men to Christian women, many of whom converted into Judaism, very few of the non-Jews marrying Jewish men and women today convert into Judaism. The same cultural tolerance that nurtures mixed marriage also promotes the idea that each partner can maintain his or her own distinctive, pre-marriage identity. Thus, the homes they are forming include two religious identities, and often two or more ethnic identities.

Today, reservations about mixed marriage carry the odor of demanding that Romeo and Juliet choose between the Montagues and the Capulets. Compared to prior social expectations, relatively few contemporary Americans believe that ethnic and religious choices are necessary, because American culture encourages individuals and families to combine multiple heritages. Americans share in the festive events and symbols of many cultures: on St. Patrick's Day, Americans can all be a "little bit Irish" through the "wearin' of the green." Eastern religious strategies are incorporated into Western lives through yoga and meditation tapes. Protestant churches sponsor Seder programs for their congregants. Unlike societies in previous historical periods and in less tolerant countries today, marriage across ethnic and religious lines is not automatically viewed as apostasy or cultural betrayal. Jews can marry

Christians without the baptism of one or the circumcision of the other. Intermarriages are viewed by many as doubling, rather than diminishing, the family's cultural capital.

American Jewish resistance to intermarriage has been replaced in recent years by the view that intermarriage is normative. The great majority of American Jews believe that intermarriage is inevitable in an open society, and fewer than half actively oppose such marriages, according to a study published in 2000 by the American Jewish Committee. When asked whether "it would pain me if my child married a gentile," only 39 percent of American Jews agreed with this statement, including 84 percent of Orthodox, 57 percent of Conservative, 27 percent of Reform, and 19 percent of "Just Jewish" respondents. Of Jews who said that Jewishness was "very important" to their lives, only 54 percent said their child's marriage to a non-Jew would be a source of pain.[5]

Facts and Figures on Intermarriage among American Jews

"Facts" and figures about levels of intermarriage are not as easy to come by as one might expect, because how one defines "mixed marriage" is affected first of all by whom one counts as a Jew. For example, should a person with one Jewish parent who was raised with no religious identification, belief, or activity except for cultural Christian observances be computed within the Jewish population? Should that person's status as a sociological (as opposed to a halakhic) Jew be affected by whether the Christian parent was a father or a mother? What category should persons who were raised in two religious traditions—Jewish and something else—be placed in? Sociologists argue over these categorizations at least as much as rabbis do, and these disputes have complicated data collection as well as analysis.

Despite these complications and uncertainties, sweeping patterns are apparent, based on the year 1990 and year 2000 National Jewish Population Surveys.[6] Close to half of the "Jewish" marriages in the years 1984–1989 were mixed marriages. Social scientists argue over whether the mixed-marriage rate during that time period was as high as 52 percent or as low as 43 percent, depending on who is counted as a Jew. All agree that mixed-marriage rates climbed precipitously during the 1970s and 1980s. According to the 1990 NJPS, slightly less than one-third (31 percent) of all mixed-married households with one Jewish parent reported that they were raising their children as Jews.

The 2000–2001 NJPS data have many logistical complications, but large trends are evident. The younger the Jew, the less gender is a factor. Among all Jews, 33 percent of men and 29 percent of women are married to non-Jews (table 5). Among Jews age fifty and over, 27 percent of men and 19 percent of women are married to non-Jews. In contrast, among Jews age twenty-five to forty-nine, 40 percent of men and 40 percent of women are married to non-Jews (table 9). The children of mixed-married households are overwhelmingly more likely to be mixed married themselves than the children of inmarried households. Thus, among twenty-five to forty-nine year olds who were raised in mixed-married households, well over three-quarters (79 percent) are also mixed married, compared to 28 percent who grew up in inmarried households (table 6). When asked what religion they currently consider themselves to be, 61 percent of twenty-five to forty-nine year olds who grew up in mixed-married households do not consider themselves to be Jewish. In contrast, only 7 percent who grew up in inmarried households do not consider themselves to be Jewish (table 8).

One indicator of the family's Jewish identification is that nearly half of mixed-married couples ages twenty-five to forty-nine said that they are raising their (randomly selected) child as a Jew: 39 percent said their child was being raised "Jewish," 8 percent reported "Jewish connected, including Jewish and some other religion," and 53 percent said the child was "not being raised Jewish." Within inmarried households, not surprisingly, 97 percent of children were being raised "exclusively Jewish" (table 7).

Some observers of the Jewish community assert that mixed-married families represent a net gain for the Jewish community—or at least an opportunity for Jewish exploration. They note that when two Jews marry, only one married household is created, whereas when a Jew marries a non-Jew, two "Jewish" households can be counted, one for each Jew involved. Were all the children raised in these mixed-married households to identify as Jews and to grow up to create new Jewish homes of their own, the reasoning goes, the American Jewish community would actually experience a communal and population increase as a result of mixed marriage. According to this view, the cultural intermingling epitomized by mixed marriage does not necessarily warrant anxiety or alarm and may even be a cause for celebration.

Similarly, some social scientists suggest that we are simply witnessing transformations in the meaning of ethnic and religious identities, rather than their dissolution. In past decades, scholars such as Andrew Greeley, Daniel Moynihan, Marcus Hansen, and others have been surprised by a resurgence of interest in ethnic identification.[7] Michael Novak argued that the transformed, enlightened ethnicities that have emerged benefit themselves and America.[8]

Nevertheless, despite the great and obvious advantages of tolerance and pluralism in American society, some observers worry about the impact of mixed marriage on Jews and Judaism. Demographers argue about how many Jews—or potential Jews—live in America, and even about how to count them. Some say that the number of Jews is far larger than has been previously estimated.[9] Many others say recent research shows that the proportion of Jews in America is static, and probably falling, pointing out that the stagnation of the Jewish population arises from several converging facts. First, relatively small numbers of Jews emigrate to the United States today, compared to other population groups, so immigration is no longer a substantial source of increased Jewish population. Second, American Jews have low levels of reproduction. Like other well-educated, ambitious white Americans, increasing numbers of Jews in their thirties have not yet married. Like others in their socioeconomic cohort, Jews tend to marry late and have their children, if any, even later. This pattern of delayed marriage and childbearing has resulted in a fertility rate demographers consider well below the 2.2 children per family replacement level. Third, increasing numbers of Americans of Jewish descent regard themselves as secular, or Jewish but not by religion.

Grateful to America for providing historically unprecedented hospitality to Jews and Judaism, some observers nonetheless regard mixed marriage as symptomatic of a cultural malaise that may weaken American Jewish vitality. Historian Jonathan Sarna recalls that "New York City's French Huguenots, to take an extreme case, married non-Huguenots between 1750 and 1769 at a rate that exceeded 86 percent" and had soon intermarried out of existence in the liberal American environment.[10] The Jews of Kaifeng, China, similarly intermarried into oblivion.[11] These historical models suggest that over time intermarriage contributes to the intermingling and gradual disappearance of meaningful distinctions between ethnic Americans and the rich and complex religious and cultural traditions they are heirs to. In a country where activists lobby on behalf of endangered species of plant and animal life, some argue, American Jewish leaders have a responsibility to vigorously enhance the survivability of the Jewish cultural and religious heritage. As Sarna puts it, if liberal Americans worry about "saving the whale," surely they should be sympathetic to those Jews who are concerned about preserving the historical Jewish civilization as well.[12]

These two scenarios, one of flourishing interfaith communities, the other of Jewish ethnoreligious disappearance, present divergent projections into the future. Put in the starkest terms (and to paraphrase numerous Jewish jokes), can today's mixed marriage be good for the Jews? Will the blessings of American openness cause Jewish culture to be virtually loved out of existence in twenty-first-century America?

Some concerned observers insist that pluralism, non-coercive as it may be, is just a different route to assimilation.[13] Deriding the new celebration of "symbolic ethnicity," for example, Herbert Gans categorizes most ethnoreligious renaissance as a shallow, nostalgic appropriation of the symbols of the past, with no deep or transformative value for individuals or their American societies. Gans argues that the ultimate poverty of symbolic ethnicity is exposed by the structural pressures of mixed marriage:

> As intermarriage continues, the number of people with parents from the same secular ethnic group will continue to decline, and by the time the fourth generation of the old immigration reaches adulthood, such people may be in a minority. . . . How would the son of an Italian mother and Irish father who has married a woman of Polish-German ancestry determine his ethnicity, and what would he and his wife tell their children . . . how would they rank or synthesize their backgrounds?

Gans further points out that "these questions are empirical, and urgently need to be studied."[14]

Despite the timeliness of this debate, however, relatively little systematic research on the internal dynamics of the interfaith family has been published. Most available research until now has been survey (population) research. Such statistical research does not, by its nature, deal with the subtleties of ethnoreligious family dynamics. Survey research excels at providing us with a snapshot in time, but it is less successful at exploring nuanced processes over time, such as the process through which families negotiate their ethnoreligious identity.

Jewishness blends sacred/religious with secular/ethnic characteristics. To be Jewish can be viewed as belonging to a religion, to a people, or both—as it has been historically. Although the number of American mixed-married Jewish households has multiplied exponentially during the past three decades, and discussion and speculation have flourished, systematic scientific research on ethnoreligious negotiations has appeared only sporadically. Most notably Bruce Phillips, along with Egon Mayer and Rela Geffen, Peter Medding, Steven Cohen, and others have raised intriguing questions.[15] The book also draws on pioneering work on ethnoreligious identity formation among non-Jewish populations, such as studies by Mary Waters, Richard Alba, and others.[16]

Double or Nothing? Jewish Families and Mixed Marriage takes up their questions and draws on hundreds of pages of original interview data to examine the day-to-day realities of family life. This discussion is based on interview data from 254 interviews conducted in sixty-eight mixed-married, thirty-six inmarried, and twenty-three conversionary families in Denver, New Jersey, Atlanta, and New England, and on four focus group discussions with teenagers growing up in interfaith families. This research, commissioned by the American Jewish Committee in New York, (see note 3) is one of the first systematic qualitative studies of the full range of mixed-married family types: Jewishly identified, two religions, secular or no formal religion, overtly Christian, and principled nontheists. The interviews, conducted between 1999–2000, focused on ongoing negotiations and renegotiations of the ethnic and religious character of mixed-married households. Households were identified by the New York survey research firm of Schulman, Ronca, & Bucuvalas, Inc. (SRBI), using a multiplicity sampling technique.

Unlike survey research, which tends to provide a snapshot in time, my goal in conducting interviews was to explore process, personal and familial evolutions, and change. The interviews and focus group discussions were recorded and professionally transcribed, and then underwent two kinds of analysis: The transcripts were coded using AFTER qualitative research software, which enabled us to create a quantified, panoramic picture of the interview data. In addition, and perhaps most important, we devoted long sessions to "immersion" reading—and rereading—transcripts of the interviews, listening to the voices of individuals, paying special attention to repeating patterns and to differences in particular family types.

Using these interviews, Parts I and II of this book explore questions such as how do one Jewish and one Christian parent decide on the religious profile of the family they are creating? What do their choices mean to them? Does a decision in favor of one or the other religion—or both or none—create tensions in the household? How do families deal with the calendar of yearly holidays, and with life cycle events? How do children view and feel about their parents' religious decisions, and how do they construct their own ethno-religious identity? How much do ethnic and cultural considerations influence familial feelings about religion? How do grandparents and other extended family members enter into the process of negotiations and renegotiations? In the interview data, husbands, wives, and their teenage children share ambivalent feelings about Judaism, Christianity, and organized religion, and reflect on their reasons for trying to incorporate ethnic culture, religious ritual, or spiritual outlets into their personal and family lives.

While these family stories are intensely personal, they convey important information about American society as a whole, and about the evolving place of Jews and other minorities in America today. Part III places Jewish mixed marriage into cultural contexts. It begins by discussing changing profiles and meanings of transethnic romances in literature and film. Romantic love has long been used as a metaphor for universalism over tribalism, and for the right of each individual to direct his or her own destiny. In the United States, stories about mixed marriage were popular in literature, drama, and film long before intermarriage became a widespread sociological phenomenon. Portrayals of mixed marriage among Jews and other ethnic and religious groups have become ubiquitous in American culture and reveal much about social change. Part III then documents the distinctive concerns and activities of this newly prominent group by looking at the programs, organizations, books, and cultural artifacts being created for them. These products provide a kind of infrastructure for mixed-married households, which in certain ways comprise a social network or kind of "virtual" society. Although they do not necessarily reside in close proximity to each other, many mixed-married families gravitate to similar activities and organizations that cater to their needs. Finally, the concluding section considers the issues precipitating controversy and Jewish communal responses to the phenomenon of mixed marriage and wrestles with the tension between the human dimensions of family formation, the American value system, and a consideration of what this changed landscape means for the future of American Jewish life.

Throughout, *Double or Nothing?* works with contemporary understandings of ethnoreligious identity construction. Concepts such as race, ethnicity, and religious difference, which once seemed determining and solidly significant factors in people's lives, are today regarded as "a matter not of essence but of choices," a voluntary and perhaps even an "artificial" construct.[17] It is the individual, rather than the group, who decides what his or her affiliation—or lack of affiliation—with a particular group may mean. Individuals also differ in their interpretations of the character and significance of the social groups themselves. Thus, even one's interpretation of a religious community and its requirements becomes a matter of individual, personal preference.[18]

During the past century, cultural historians have transformed the way communal stories are interpreted. Rather than depicting the evolution of a particular national, ethnic, or religious group as "a grand narrative in which the many individuals are submerged," some currently influential methods focus on the "micro" picture, a multiplicity of small stories, "a multifaceted flow with many individual centers."[19] *Double or Nothing?* follows this approach, using the particularized stories of interview participants to illuminate the broader psychosocial dimensions of mixed marriage. This approach is often referred to as "thick description," the documentation and analysis of social change through myriad small details, as advocated by cultural anthropologist Clifford Geertz.[20] I analyze the texts provided by diverse individual stories, as each of the informants have interpreted their own lives, behaviors, and goals. I am especially interested in the ways in which husbands and wives negotiate the ethnic and religious character of their households, the ways in which these negotiations change over time, and the impact of extended family members and friends on these continuing negotiations.

My informants described both life-transforming moments and quotidian daily, weekly, and yearly routines. I asked them not only what they did but also how they interpret events and decisions in their own lives. Sometimes my interpretations of informants' lives, as I analyze them in a research context, differ from the ways in which they understand themselves. When ethnoreligious societies seemed relatively defined and stable, social scientists measured characteristics through formally defined yardsticks, often derived from the behaviors and attitudes that had characterized these particular societies in the past. However, today, in our times of enormous societal flux, it is much less clear what particular behaviors may mean—and what their significance is to the individuals, families, and societies who do or do not perform them.

Semiotics, or the meaning of behaviors—rather than the behaviors themselves—is often a primary focus of exploration within the social sciences today. Society, and the "social structures and processes that were seen as the determinants of a society . . . are now increasingly viewed rather as products of culture."[21] Cultures are themselves defined by networks of meanings in some ways not appreciably different from those in a literary text. Geertz articulates this hypothesis: "Man is an animal suspended in webs of significance he himself has spun. I take culture to be those webs, and the analysis of it to be therefore not an experimental science in search of law but an interpretive one in search of meaning."[22]

Mixed-married couples have unprecedented opportunities to "invent traditions" for their households as well as themselves, to borrow Eric Hobsbawm's useful phrase.[23] Before they marry and then as they create their new families, mixed-married couples are free to determine the ethnoreligious character, if any, of their homes. These negotiations continue for the life of the couple's relationship, not only before but sometimes beyond the life of the marriage. Indeed, although divorced couples are not the purview of this study, negotiations about the children's religious identity frequently continue with renewed vigor after divorce.

The fluidity of ethnoreligious identity in American Jewish households—especially mixed-married households—has long been an understudied psychosocial dynamic. Based on my original interview research in which participants describe how and why their families have changed over time, *Double Or Nothing?* is one of the first systematic studies focusing on the process of mixed-married couples negotiating their identity as individuals and as families. I suggest that these familial psychosocial travelogues have a larger cultural significance that often parallels the "fictional" stories that foreshadow, echo, and reflect social change. I argue that the growing prominence of mixed-married families has helped to create a new social reality, in which the previously pro-endogamy (inmarriage) bias of American society has given way to a largely pro-exogamy (outmarriage) ethos. I show how these pro-exogamy trends have transformed American Jewish communal norms, and even the way Jews understand and talk about their ancient texts and historical experiences. These personal, individual stories of American Jewish mixed-married families, along with my analysis of their meaning, cultural sources, and impact, now become texts themselves for a scholarly and broader cultural discussion.

I

THROUGH THE
LOOKING GLASS

1

WHEN OPPOSITES ATTRACT

The Way We Were

This portrait of mixed-married American Jewish families begins with inter-view participants' memories of their homes, neighborhoods, schools, and friendship groups during their childhood and teen years, which they spoke of avidly. The readiness with which informants talked about the past, and the salience that they appeared to discover in their own narratives, should not be surprising. Stories about one's own past grip individuals powerfully from childhood ("tell me a story about when I was little") through every stage of adult experience. Family groups and ethnic communities, as well as individ-uals, often utilize memory narratives to help them understand their current situations and chart future directions.

The more extensive the transformations they have experienced, the more people and societies may rely on factual or mythic retellings of their own *bil-dungsroman* to give them a sense of continuity with their roots. For inter-view participants, as for many Americans navigating the unpredictable flux of current lifestyles, it seemed deeply meaningful to reflect on earlier periods of life. For those recalling a stable childhood and teen years, their memories comprised a kind of psychic village, filled with friends and acquaintances as well as parents, grandparents, and other relatives who knew their families, their streets, their youthful escapades. Even participants whose early years included greater elements of disruption and pain said they found it useful to talk about their pasts.

Many spoke about how their childhood homes were linked to the homes they are creating today, and the ways in which their own personal transformations reflect wider social change. They drew on and analyzed connections between their past and present experiences, talking about the forces that had shaped them and contributed to their eventual choice of marital partner.

The stories our informants told were diverse, but they were also linked by how *American* they were. Most interview participants had American parents; the majority of both Jewish and non-Jewish participants also had at least one or two American grandparents. For a shrinking number of American Jews, communal memories stretch backward to Old Country origins, to immigration, and to social re-establishment. For most Jews, however, even the old, remembered neighborhoods and lifestyles are Americanized and multiethnic, as increasing proportions of Jews are fourth- and fifth-generation Americans. Interestingly, those mixed-married Jewish participants who had personally emigrated tended to be married to non-Jewish immigrants.

Stories told by mixed-married spouses about their growing up years included several strikingly similar themes. *Not every mixed-married spouse had each characteristic,* but the vast majority described one or more of the following personal characteristics: (1) most Jewish and non-Jewish participants characterized themselves as being very "independent" from or "different" than the family and community they had grown up in; (2) many Jewish participants characterized their homes and communities as "too materialistic"; (3) Jewish participants often reported that their homes provided weak or no religious grounding, saying they had minimal or no formal religious education, or that their parents had not supported the religious education they did receive; or they called their parents religiously "hypocritical," or "inconsistent"; (4) many non-Jewish participants said that their parents had converted between Christian denominations or otherwise changed religious affiliations over the years; (5) most Jewish and non-Jewish participants said that they had many friends from another religious group, and/or that they found the home life or the religious life of friends from another religious group attractive; (6) many Jewish and non-Jewish participants said that as teenagers they found their own religion irrational, too repressive, or in some other way unappealing; (7) about one in four non-Jewish participants characterized their childhood homes as dysfunctional households, talking about cold, indifferent parents, or excessive mobility, or a painful divorce, or alcoholism, sometimes accompanied by abusive behavior.

I Did It My Way

A deep sense of personal uniqueness was expressed by almost every participant. Significantly, each person characterized him/herself as "different" and distinct from others they had encountered over the years. This conviction of uniqueness was accompanied by an almost limitless sense of freedom and opportunity. Unaware of the ways in which their choices were embedded in the values of successive social networks, individuals spoke with evident satisfaction about following their hearts to their own individual destinies, both in terms of their ambitions and their romantic choices. The perceived openness of their choices of what they might study, where they might live, and whom they might marry confirmed their American birthright.

Early ethnic, cultural, or religious experiences, whether through parental home-based celebrations and rituals, synagogue experiences, or formal Jewish education, had a durable, if often belated, affect during the evolution of the individual, and later the mixed-married family, as we will see in more detail in part II. Once general background considerations were taken into account, individual preferences turned out to be a very important key as to how our respondents experienced the religious character of the homes from which they came. The significance of individual leanings was particularly striking when we interviewed siblings. Each sibling grows up in a different family in certain ways. This is true not only because parental attitudes or circumstances can change but also because each child is different and responds to different stimuli.

Some siblings remembered that, even as children, they were attracted to religiosity, while others remembered shying away from it. For example, Judy Yadegar, who later chose to marry a Jew, remembered, "I always liked my grandmother. She was very religious. I used to love to go over there on Friday night. We used to sit and talk about everything. She was a big influence on me." However, her brother, Jason, who later married a non-Jewish woman, had a strikingly different memory: "I was very close to my grandfather. He was a deeply secular person—very bright and skeptical and interesting. We spent a lot of time together. We saw the world in very similar ways."

Thus, even within one happily remembered family, people who as children were attracted to religiosity often responded to and sought out religious relatives, while those with other interests found relatives who could nurture those aspects of their lives. Of course, it is also entirely possible that these data reveal selective memory: those who choose a particular path remember those grandparents whom they believe would have approved of their choices.

Being romantically involved with a non-Jew provides a Jew with a powerful tool for expressing individuation and separation from parents. Interfaith romance as a symbol of individuation is a pattern that can emerge early. Joel Millstein, a Jewish musician married to a highly cultured Presbyterian woman, said, "I didn't try to be rebellious, but I need to do things my way. I mean all through high school, college, and even today. The things I do rankle my parents at times. I didn't go out of my way to stick it in their faces necessarily. It was just, this is who I was." Millstein remembered being powerfully attracted to the world of music—and to non-Jewish young women—even before his bar mitzvah:

> I had some pretty serious girlfriends. They were all musical, and only one was Jewish, which scared my parents. Because I wasn't going to grow up to have a Jewish life, a Jewish house. When I was twelve, my father said to me, "If you marry someone who's not Jewish our relationship will change forever." We were walking to *shul* [synagogue]. And he wanted to make sure. And he didn't say not Jewish, he said Christian.

To please their parents, young people who are attracted to romantic partners from other religions sometimes start by dating—or even marrying— someone from their own religious background. However, they often sabotage these in-faith relationships by picking a person they can never be happy with, and then, predictably, ending that relationship, as Millstein did: "I knew Jewish girls at Hebrew school. Didn't like them. The first in my string of pretty girlfriends was Jewish. I met her at summer camp. And she was really certifiably unstable. And so I didn't continue in that direction. . . ." When the pre-doomed endogamous relationship predictably goes up in smoke, they proceed to pursue interfaith romances, relishing the independence they enable and represent. Joel Millstein's tale merged "foreign" girls and interests and activities in his demonstration to his parents that he was his own man:

In college I met a girl from Kentucky. That was my first serious girlfriend. And that just freaked them [his parents] out, because I mean that's really foreign!

I was a musician and the son of a very practical, pragmatic businessman. I went out with non-Jewish girls. Got pretty serious with this one. Went to the midwest. Got involved in just lifestyles that were foreign to them. . . .

The teacher I got the first year in Indiana was from Salzburg. He asked me if I wanted to come back and study with him.

INT: How did your parents feel about that?

Terrible! About the same as they felt when I bought my very first French horn from my teacher, and my father went to the airport to pick it up, and he had to pay a duty because it came from Germany. And this was fifteen years after World War II. He was ashen-faced. But I didn't really think about it. . . .

I actually went to Austria in September of 1972, two hours away from Munich where the Olympics were going on at the same time. And I think they thought I was a lost cause. With a non-Jewish girl, living together and not married, in Austria, studying with a German. A lot farther away from Indiana. All of a sudden it made Indiana look pretty close to home.

No Place Like Home

Jewish and non-Jewish participants both talked about how they had used friendships and romantic liaisons across ethnic and religious lines to rebel against their families. These personal stories of intercultural love as a vehicle for rebellion and independence from controlling Jewish parents were often similar in many ways to novels and films about love across ethnoreligious barriers, as we will see in chapter 8. Like decades of portrayals of Jews as relentlessly materialistic, in my study, Jewish participants who deliberately sought out spouses from non-Jewish—and thus exotic—backgrounds, complained often and extensively about their Jewish homes and communities being too materialistic.

Materialism was a charge repeatedly leveled at Jewish families. Socioeconomic issues embedded in ethnoreligious considerations, and couched in a kind of neurotic obsession with material success, was part of the standard parental "speech" about dating Jews, according to many mixed-married Jewish participants. As one man reported, marrying Jewish was heavily tied into a kind of bourgeois package that included the Jewish girl, her parents' money, a professional career direction, etc. This Jewish-girl-as-a-middle-class-norm undercut the significance of a Jewish marriage as a value in and of itself. By marrying a Jewish princess, he could become himself a "crown" prince: "You know, the standard parental thing. How did they express it? My mother was sort of a social climber, so she was always—she always had this fantasy of finding some, you know, wealthy Jewish princess or something, I think. That would sort of—what's the word—serendipitously elevate her status somehow. Marry a Crown."

Another described his parents' directives as a Jewish version of the all-American dream: "I knew what they wanted. They wanted me to be a doctor and they wanted me to marry a Jewish girl and they wanted me to have two-and-a-half kids and have a picket fence and probably live in another two-family house right next door to their house."

According to their memories, many mixed-married Jews became conscious of materialistic aspects of American Jewish life when they were very young. In some cases, a move to a more affluent, gentile neighborhood triggered their feelings that Jews were both too different and too bourgeois. Many remembered feeling tension between materialistic success, accompanied by assimilation to American middle-class mores, and individual integrity. As Joellen Masterson recalled:

> My parents were raised in Roxbury and Dorchester, Jewish ghettos. And it was a very big deal to move to Belmont, because Belmont was not a very Jewish community. My parents had broken out of the ghetto, but they faced some antisemitism. My father was the first person in his family to go to college.
>
> We did not keep a kosher household. High holidays we had very prestigious seats in the first row of the auditorium. My father I think was president at one time of that temple. . . . I was very into the liturgy. I sat with my father and played with the strings on his *talit* [prayershawl] and raced through the prayers with him to see who could say them the fastest and loudest.
>
> All of my parents' friends were Jewish. I remember as a child having a lot of pressure to have Jewish friends—which was a little hard in Belmont since there were only a few Jewish kids there, and I wasn't too keen on them.
>
> I remember feeling a lot of alienation with the Jewish community because I thought that they were a fairly materialistic group, country clubs, golf, fancy houses. They were a generation that had grown up in the Depression. Being Depression kids to them meant making a success by having a good job and liv-

ing in a nice place was really the hallmark of a successful life for my parents' generation. And then that was sort of followed by retirement in Florida.

That was what my father stood for but not my mother. My mother had been a socialist in college. She was a practicing social worker. And she gave up her career to have her children, and then she virtually gave up most of the things she believed in. . . . Later she found a way to reclaim it. She had a kind of subversive rebellion.

Jewishness perceived as a consumer, middle-class culture was an extremely common attitude among Jews who married non-Jews. Many associated growing up Jewish with a sense of having limited sociological and psychological options, of feeling hemmed in by bourgeois proprieties.

Joellen also reacted to what she perceived as the comfortably middle-class, critical and neurotic but not particularly spiritual or religious, environment of her Jewish household by seeking out non-Jewish boyfriends from beyond her college experience at Brandeis University:

I had a lot of boyfriends. My freshman year I met somebody at a mixer who was a graduate student at MIT, also not Jewish . . . then my second year I had a boyfriend who was Jewish who was a year younger than me at Brandeis, but I didn't feel that he was motivated in life or so serious about it. And then in my last two years at Brandeis I kind of dated around. And had a good time. And most of the people that I hung out with and slept with were my good friends, there was sort of a crowd of us, and most of them were Jewish. But Judaism didn't play any part in those relationships except in the cultural sense. . . .

When I graduated from Brandeis I hung out again with that high school boyfriend from Framingham for a year. Then I met another guy, and I was in touch with Patrick. He was in Vietnam. . . . Then there was this guy named Paul, also not Jewish, that I hung out with. I hung out with a lot of guys who were not Jewish, working class guys. They were sort of underachievers and came from really totally different backgrounds from mine. And we didn't really have that much in common when it came right down to it. I am sure that is why I never married any of them. Paul and I took acid together—that was a very strong religious experience of sorts! . . .

Caleb was a bicycle racer. . . . He has all along been fairly indifferent about religious practice because he considers himself an atheist. Caleb's parents are great! They are so normal—which was different from my experience in which nobody was normal. They seemed to love each other and make everybody feel good.

Interfaith romances enabled Jews to feel that they had more open horizons. In their own words, contemplating marriage to a Christian man or woman made them feel adventurous. By choosing a non-Jew, and perhaps transgressing the wishes of their parents and other family or community members, they said they felt freer. Marrying a non-Jew became symbolic of their non-conformity to what Joel Millstein called "Jewish stifling expectations."

Non-Jews who married Jews also sometimes remembered looking for friends and lovers who could help them rebel against the environment in which they grew up. Friendship groups played pivotal roles during the teen years and in college as these patterns were established. My study shows that high school friendship groups are a very strong predictor of college friendship groups, in terms of how many Jews one tends to socialize with. For teenagers, and then for college students and young adults, these friendship groups form a primary social network. The values that each individual comes to consider unique to him or her are embedded in their social network.[1] Thus, not surprisingly, having many friends of another faith was often a precursor to picking a spouse of that same faith. Several non-Jewish interview participants said Jews were attractive to them because Jews are intellectual or politically liberal. Many spoke of "discovering" Jewish friends in high school, then seeking out Jewish friends in college as well, and finally marrying a Jew.

For example, Chad Marquardt, who grew up in what he describes as "a rigid Lutheran home," said he rebelled against his parents' devoutness by becoming involved in "drugs and loud music" as a young teenager. However, when he was a junior in high school he became very friendly with and spent hours in the home of a Jewish boy. He said he was astonished to see that his Jewish friend's parents "read books and listened to classical music and argued loudly about politics at the dinner table." After a few months of experiencing this dramatically different family style, he "gave up [his] wild friends" and took up almost exclusively with "intellectual Jewish friends in high school and college." Ultimately, in keeping with his friendship patterns, Chad married a Jewish woman.

Similarly, Jerry Goldberg, whose wife, Charlene, eventually converted into Judaism, said that "for her there was a sort of romance about finding the real East Coast Jewish intellectual—in the person of me!" Goldberg spoke eloquently about Charlene's attraction to Jewish liberal attitudes, open ideas, and the active role that Jewish women have played in feminist causes:

As I understand her personal journey, she was pretty alienated from the Catholic religion of her youth. My wife's a pretty practical, this-world person anyway. . . . I think that especially over women's issues, she felt far from the Catholic church because she's a strong feminist, a strong believer in birth control, a strong believer in abortion rights. And a strong believer in the equality of women—which, as a matter of fact, gave her a fair amount of difficulty with Judaism too!

She had come East from Seattle to go to school in Newark, because she was attracted to the idea of New York in her head. She read the *New Yorker* from an early age. . . . She had this image, which I don't know if she consciously thought of it as being Judaic, but the New York intellectual scene and the New York art scene has always included a lot of Jews. . . .

She liked the contrast to Catholicism and the other varieties of Christianity, the relative openness of Judaism to debate, exchange of ideas, questioning even the most basic of doctrines. And I think she liked the idea that a lot of the feminists she admired came from Jewish backgrounds. . . . She kind of liked that Jewish women were more openly in the revolt against the patriarchal aspects of the religion. . . .

For an important minority of this study's informants, mixed marriage seemed to be a strategy of remaking their lives so that they wouldn't repeat painful patterns they observed in the homes they grew up in. One woman pithily remarked, "My mother was a dysfunctional person who brought unhappiness to herself and everyone who lived in her household. I have tried very hard not to do anything the way my mother did it."

Among mixed-married couples, a substantial group remembered the homes they had grown up in as being dysfunctional in some way. More than one in four non-Jews and almost one in five Jews who married someone of a different faith reported parental coldness, alcoholism, excessive mobility, verbal or violent abuse, and occasionally sexual dysfunctions. It should be emphasized that this pattern occurred among a minority of our sample population. Nevertheless, memories of childhood family dysfunctions were disproportionately represented among the mixed-married informants, compared to those who married within their own faith.

Strikingly, men and women who said they came from dysfunctional families often spoke strongly about seeking out a spouse whose home life was emphatically different from their own. Among the most dramatic stories was that of Kara Mermelstein, who described her upper-class "Brahmin" Protestant family as rife with dysfunctions. "The last thing I wanted was a family like the one I grew up in," she said, after relating a youth that included incestuous relationships in an otherwise cool and uninvolved familial environment. She noted bitterly, "Jewish mothers and their families may be controlling, but at least they care where you are. My family never tried to control me because they were too wrapped up in themselves and never cared enough to make it their business."

Aside from the pronounced American flavor of their recollections, both Jewish and non-Jewish interview and focus group participants spanned a broad gamut of background experiences. They came from different kinds of neighborhoods: some matured within the sophistication of exclusive sections of Manhattan and private schools; others grew up in rough, declining urban areas and learned early how to defend themselves in schoolyard fights. Some Jews had been part of only a handful of Jews in smallish southern, midwestern, or western towns, while others had been surrounded by so many Jews in their public schools that Jewishness seemed safe—and boring. Non-Jewish respondents included those raised in diverse Protestant denominations, some families devout, others secularized; a good number came from Catholic homes, some lapsed, others strictly observant. Some remembered the firm structures of one organized religious orientation, while others recalled continual religious change: families that experimented with Catholic, Baptist, Mormon, and Buddhist faiths. Among the Jewish respondents, a few descended from families that had fought in the Civil War, while some had been born outside the United States; this group included some children of Holocaust survivors. A sprinkling were raised as Christians and discovered only in adolescence that they had a Jewish parent or grandparent.

Romantic choices had an impact on not only the man and woman who decided to link their destinies but also their parents, siblings, extended families, and friends. Conversely, the decisions of individuals concerning whom and when to marry are influenced in some obvious ways, and many more subtle ways, by their relationships with family and friends over the years. Not least, as couples think about the possibility of marrying and constructing a new household together, the realities of the homes they grew up in often lurk at the back of their minds, either as positive role models—or as paradigms they try hard not to repeat.

Most informants spoke of caring, responsible parents, and many had close relationships with grandparents and other relatives. Within these positive memories there were many variations. The majority of both Jewish and non-Jewish informants remember traditionally structured households: fathers who spent most of their time as breadwinners, and mothers who devoted themselves to homemaking and communal good works. In such households, the power structure was often conventionally divided as well: fathers made major decisions about money and family moves, while mothers dealt with day-to-day choices and crises. A substantial minority, however, recalled mothers who worked outside the home, some of whom were professionals or artists, as well as other, less conventional household arrangements. Some of their mothers went back to school and/or worked as they grew up, bringing familial change in their wake. Because of their age group (twenty-five to fifty-five), many of our informants were children in the 1960s and 1970s in households that navigated their way through the transitional phase of second-wave feminist change in America.

More Than Chemistry

Although the choice of a partner or spouse often appears to be the purest example of individual freedom, our interviews corroborate the strong relationship between certain background experiences and the likelihood that a person will marry someone of a different faith. Among Jews, the likelihood of inmarriage is greatly enhanced by several factors, including but not limited to growing up in a home with many types of Jewish activities, such as religious rituals and ceremonies and cultural connections; receiving a substantial level of Jewish education, especially through the teenage years; and having significant numbers of Jewish friends during the teenage years. It should be noted that each of these factors involves social interactions.

Ethnic and religious considerations come into play for both those who marry within their own ethnic and faith tradition and for those who marry out. For inmarriers, similarity of background and values carried a potent erotic charge. Although some inmarried couples said they had been influenced by concern about Jewish continuity issues and had thought about the fact that the creation of Jewish households facilitates coherent cultural transmission from one generation to the next, they mainly wanted to marry their Jewish spouses because they found them attractive and because "S/he was so much like me!" In other words, Jews didn't marry Jews because they felt a sense of duty to the Jewish community, but because they loved the Jewish individuals they married!

Arguably, part of the reason they were attracted to those particular individuals had to do with the internalization of positive associations with characteristics perceived as being "Jewish." However, for those men and women who fall in love with and marry individuals with different backgrounds, difference—rather than similarity—itself is part of the attraction.

There are a number of reasons why some individuals may be drawn toward romantic relationships with people who derive from divergent ethnoreligious heritages. Some Jews had ambivalent feelings about identifying exclusively with the Jewish people. Many mixed-married Jewish informants recounted uncomfortable recollections about their high school years, including a shy or painful adolescence; being "always different from the rest of my family"; or saying they were "always rebellious" against what they described as the constraining norms of their communities or families.

Some said they remembered feeling angry about the fact that their religious/ethnic identity made them feel unpleasantly distinctive. Some were still resentful about antisemitic remarks as they were growing up. One woman, for example, talked about being self-conscious about the kind of sandwiches she brought to school, on challah or whole wheat instead of white bread. She hated being different and being ridiculed. "I didn't look Jewish, not a bit!" Gena Monroe remembered, "And my name—Gena Gerson—didn't sound particularly Jewish either." The idea of "passing" as a non-Jew occurred to her early, particularly because she found growing up as a Jew painful. She liked the idea of being part of the majority culture as a girl and a teenager, and she often saw Christian identity as a way of escaping her embarrassing Jewish difference. Now, as a Jew married to a Christian, Gena says she enjoys participating in and identifying with both religious traditions: "It is hard growing up Jewish, because almost everybody else is Christian, and it would be easier to be Christian. And then a lot of times I was embarrassed or ashamed [to be Jewish], and I thought, oh God, it would be so much better if I was just Christian. But now that I have gotten older, I wouldn't give up my Judaism for anything. So, you know."

Although many observers assume that Israeli culture breeds rugged self-esteem, some children of immigrants from Israel expressed a squeamishness about being Jewish that sounded not unlike that of children from European Jewish immigrant families a century ago. Irit Ben-David Martinez, for ex-

ample, said that she and her siblings "cried so much" about being in a Jewish school that her parents "put us in the public school." Primarily, said Irit, "we didn't want to be different from everyone else. You know, we were different. We had the foreign parents. We wanted to be like the other kids in the neighborhood."

Like a large proportion of mixed-married Jews, Irit was deeply absorbed by sports. (One interviewer called this the "Jewish jock factor" in mixed marriage.) Irit found herself "dating all non-Jewish boys, except for one." According to her own analysis of her motivations, it was precisely the lack of common background that attracted her:

> In high school I dated this one boy. We had nothing in common. [Laughter.] Nothing. [The attraction was] probably that we had nothing in common. He was just so different. . . . And in the end, he went into the Navy. And that was the end of that.
>
> That's probably what attracted me to Carlos [her husband] as well. And he was a fun guy. Very athletic, very into sports, which I enjoy too.

Irit said that Carlos had more trouble explaining her to his Catholic family than she had explaining Carlos to her Israeli-Jewish family. She also believed it was noteworthy that she and her sister both married non-Jews, and her brother married a Christian woman who converted into Judaism.

As we explore more fully in chapter 8, mixed-married informants often had been influenced by negative cultural stereotypes of Jewish and non-Jewish personality traits. Gail Alvarez thoughtfully analyzed why she preferred non-Jewish men as romantic partners:

> You asked why I didn't date Jewish men growing up. . . . I think it has to do with my perception growing up that Jewish men were viewed by others as weak, and by my own family experience. I think my parents, as immigrants, wanted to be fully integrated into the cultural life of the country, even though they maintained a Jewish identity. I remember feeling insecure with my Jewish identity while growing up. Also, my mother always seemed to dominate in her relationship with my dad, and I recall thinking that he was a weak man, and I was so disappointed by that fact that I extended that feeling to other Jewish men.

This and other interview data from my study show how individuals are influenced not only by their own personal experiences and by the norms and values embedded in their social networks, but also by portrayals of Jewish men and women in books, films, and popular culture. Interestingly, Gail found that the reflections stimulated by the interviewing process precipitated deep discussions between her and her husband long after the interviews were completed. Eventually, she wrote to the interview team to tell them that she and he had decided that he would formally convert into Judaism.

As interview participants described the characteristics they perceived in Jewish and non-Jewish friends and spouses, they were expressing the idea that particular ethnoreligious communities have a kind of group "personality." Recent research on Catholic couples from Irish, Italian, Central European, and other mixed ethnic backgrounds demonstrates that they commonly assign particular characteristics to specific ethnic groups. Mary Waters finds that individuals are often influenced by their perceptions of their own ethnic names or looks, using them as clues as to which ethnicity they should adopt as their own. The perceived status of different ethnic groups is also an important influence, and Waters's Catholic population often adopted a particular ethnic derivation because they perceived it as being more socially acceptable or prestigious.[2]

Formal and Informal Religious Education

As a group, both Christian and Jewish participants who married across ethnoreligious lines tended to have received relatively minimal levels of religious education, although there were certainly a number of notable exceptions to this pattern. In line with data from the 1990 NJPS, the great majority of mixed-married Jews in our study had received comparatively low levels of, or no, formal (classroom) Jewish education. Mixed-married Jews were also likely to come from homes that had relatively minimal levels of Jewish ritual and ceremonial activity. Although many of them had gone to high schools with a fair number of Jews, they had not participated in youth groups, clubs, or Jewish camping experiences with other Jewish teenagers. Despite their proximity to Jews, their close friendship circles were not Jewish.

Some mixed-marrying Jews, from both affluent and poor families, were sent to Christian schools. For example, one man from a poor family went to a Catholic school in a working-class New England town, and a woman from a wealthy Manhattan home went to Episcopalian private schools.

Just the opposite pattern is true of Jews who marry other Jews and establish an unambiguously Jewish family. Jews who choose Jews have often internalized the value of creating a vibrant Jewish home during years of mutually reinforcing formal and informal Jewish educational experiences. As a group, many have received six or more years of substantial Jewish education, either day school or several days a week of supplementary school education. A large proportion of them continued their Jewish education and youth group activities through their teenage years. And, not least, the families in which inmarrying Jews grew up tended to have consistently strong attachments to Jewish rituals and communal activities, whether they took place in Orthodox, Conservative, or Reform settings.

Some Jews with extensive Jewish education and background do marry non-Jews, but they are much more likely to ask their spouses to convert, or to raise their children as Jews even if their spouses do not convert. Connecting memories of their childhood and teen years with adult decisions about how to raise their children, mixed-married Jews with strong Jewish backgrounds described a jigsaw puzzle in which they rejected some aspects of their upbringing but not others.

For example, Joel Millstein, as we have seen, was one of many Jewish men who remembered rebelling against the "bourgeois" nature of his parental home. Millstein, the son of a businessman and a "homemaker/Hadassah lady" mother, grew up in an intensely Conservative Jewish family. His reflections about himself and his family bear striking parallels to certain male characters in American Jewish novels and films, as we will note in chapter 8.

Millstein came from a "good" Jewish background. He had eight years of Jewish education and attended Jewish summer camps. Comparatively few American Jews with Millstein's profile marry out of the faith; but when they do, they often encourage their spouses to convert into Judaism. Highly educated Jewish women who marry non-Jewish men also often commit to raising their children exclusively in the Jewish faith; however, as Jewish women, they face fewer obstacles from within the community, because Orthodox and Conservative congregations usually follow rabbinic law, which considers the children of Jewish mothers bona fide Jews, regardless of the father's religion.

Millstein is characteristic in many ways of the well-educated outmarrier. He says he "respected" Carol's decision not to convert, but he insisted that each of their three children be converted into Judaism so that they would be halakhically Jewish. Millstein is looking ahead to the hoped-for marriages of their school-age children and says he wants them to be able to marry Jews and create their own Jewish homes.

Jewish outmarriers' inconsistent or ambivalent attitudes toward Jewish connections in the homes they grew up in was often linked to a profound ambivalence toward Judaism. Guy Naiman remembers thinking when he was growing up that Jewish activities were lackluster and devoid of appeal and relevance:

> What's that thing with Passover where you ask the questions? We never asked the question. You see? I don't even remember.
>
> We had the meal, but we didn't have seders per se. There was gefilte fish. There was all the traditional trimmings. Was there any religious significance given to it? No. . . . My father wasn't thrilled when I wouldn't eat matza and I was always looking for bread during Passover.

Today, Naiman says that he feels connected to Jewishness "as a cultural thing," partially because of the historical persecution of the Jews. However, this does not necessarily mean that he rejects the basic tenets of Christianity. Naiman reflected on his deep agnosticism about the possibility of assessing the truthfulness of any religion:

> Remaining Jewish to me is a very cultural thing. I honestly believe that an awful lot of people, both within my family and without, suffered so that I had the right to remain a Jew.
>
> So I stay a Jew. But if you would ask me—Carla and I have had this conversation—what do you think of Jesus Christ, I have to tell you that two thousand years ago I wasn't there.
>
> They questioned this man. The rabbis questioned Jesus. He went before a tribunal, I believe, and was asked certain questions, and the rabbis decided from what I gather that this is not the messiah. Now, is this possible? No one alive today knows. Is it possible that the rabbis said after he left, "If we just take this guy for the messiah, we're out of work!" Maybe they just denied it because it wasn't in their best interests to have this guy as the messiah.
>
> Maybe he was. Maybe we've been waiting 5,700 whatever years and the guy has been here and gone. I mean, I don't know.
>
> I say this in the kidding manner, but if you're going to accept the fact that we have a God, period, you're going to believe in God, is it possible that Jesus Christ was His son, or was the messiah? It's possible. I wasn't there. Will I accept him? . . . No, I cannot accept him. Too many people died for me to all of

a sudden make the Jews disappear, because if I start to accept him as all the Jews for Jesus do, in that event, Jews will be gone. And that's why most Jews don't want Jews to intermarry. They want Judaism to continue.

And I don't blame them. We were the first. Our ideas are the basis of Christianity. Jesus was a Jew, born a Jew, died a Jew. His last supper was the Passover seder. . . . So I disagree with some of the things that the Christian world has done with this man, Jesus, or the messiah, whoever he may be.

2

MEET MY PARENTS

Attitudes among Americans toward the possible intermarriage of their children have been transformed over the past few decades; among both Jews and non-Jews, acceptance of mixed marriage has grown. Increasing acceptance of mixed marriage was powerfully illustrated when we asked our informants to describe their teenage friendship and dating patterns, the attitudes of their parents toward their friends and dates when they lived at home, and the responses of their parents and extended family when they decided to marry their present spouses.

The homes remembered by mixed-married Jewish spouses differed in their Jewish connections from the homes remembered by inmarried Jews. The great majority of mixed-married informants said they received no parental guidance as to the persons they might date or marry. In contrast, a minority of inmarried Jews said their parents never talked about interfaith dating and marriage. Instead, inmarried Jews said parents discussed these issues with them and clearly articulated why it mattered to them that their children marry Jews and establish a Jewish home. Similarly, few mixed-married informants said their parents had expressed ambivalent or negative feelings about their choice of a spouse with a different religion, while most said their parents were positive and accepting.

Observers of the American Jewish community often attribute the rise in mixed marriage to the ubiquitous American Jewish pattern of Jewish youth attending colleges, and graduate and professional schools, away from home.

The assumption underlying this perception is that teenage Jews do not date non-Jews when they are under parental supervision, and it is only when they leave home that they initiate romantic relationships with Christian partners. However, most Jews married to non-Jews who participated in our study said they had mixed friendship groups and dating partners while they lived at home under their parents' supervision.

Perhaps most typical, informants remembered indirection in parental comments:

> My parents never, never drove us in one direction or another. Never talked about who we should date, who we should marry. If I had to guess, I think my father—it would have meant more to my father that I married a Jew than my mother. I think it meant a lot less to my mother. She always said grow up and be what you want, be happy. And her Jewish connection just was not there. With my father, though, I think—I think my father, if you pushed him, he would have said he would have preferred that we marry within the tribe, but he never did say it. But you knew he felt it.

Others commented that their parents hadn't said much about their dating because they didn't date in high school.

Perhaps surprisingly, even when mixed-married informants had contemplated college choices, few of their parents made it clear that they wanted their children to attend schools where they could meet and marry Jews, or that marrying Jews was an important family priority.

In comparison, inmarried respondents recalled their parents speaking to them about Jewish homes and Jewish values in very direct ways that were not linked to economic and social mobility issues:

> They were visibly pleased for me to have a Jewish girlfriend, bring her to dinner, bring her to Friday nights. And as it was, it had become pretty clear pretty quickly to anybody I dated that I couldn't go out Fridays, couldn't do much of anything until Saturday night. And that always means because I'm Jewish and my dad wouldn't let me out on those days and so on and so forth. Those things never lasted too long.

In contrast to these families in which resistance to interdating was part of a multifaceted, Jewishly active environment, according to many respondents, parental laissez faire attitudes, which were commonplace about their dating patterns, extended to the prospect of mixed marriage as well. Indeed, even when parents were unhappy or agitated about an upcoming mixed marriage, they did not openly encourage as yet unattached siblings to date Jews exclusively:

I had been given the "We love whoever you bring home, but if they're Jewish, then that's great too" speech several times. Having cousins who married not Jewish certainly didn't make things any easier, because every time another one would do so, it would mean that my brother and I were going to get the speech again. But there was no kind of prohibition or anything like that. My brother married a non-Jewish woman. That was—it became a bigger—well, she's actually half Jewish, but not observant at all. That became a bigger deal towards the—as their wedding approached. And kind of the same thing happened with my sister, who married a non-Jewish man. And the tension around that really grew around planning for the wedding and the ceremony and what it would be like. So it was clear that it was a preference, but it wasn't anything that they were going to push anybody on. It was never—no one ever argued, or said shouldn't you date someone else.

Because parents often did not make an issue of interdating, their dissatisfaction with the prospect of their offspring marrying a non-Jew often came as a surprise to the son or daughter in question:

My father wasn't pleased with my getting more and more serious with her. My grandmother wasn't happy. Everybody was unhappy about that. They all thought she was a nice girl and they liked her and all that but she wasn't Jewish.

INT: So what did they say?

Well, my father came out and said, "Why can't you just, why the hell do you have to do that, why can't you find somebody who is Jewish?" Everybody else didn't say anything but I heard about it afterwards, years later that they were unhappy, they liked her but they were unhappy.

The parents of the bride or groom were far less likely to object to the choice of a spouse from another faith tradition if the marriage seemed "late" to them and they were worried that their adult child would never marry. This was especially true of Jewish parents. One participant articulated the feelings of many when she said, "My father was so happy that I had a mate that he didn't care whether he was Jewish or not. He just wanted me to be settled." Families were also less likely to object when the mixed marriage was a second marriage.

Among our participants, as in the national data, mixed marriages generally involved somewhat older marriage partners than did inmarriages. In some cases, the mixed marriages took place later because partners met each other somewhat later in life. In other cases, the mixed marriage itself was an issue: the mixed-married couple had been going together or living together and took some time to decide that they wanted to proceed with marriage, despite the fact that they could not agree on a single religion in the household.

In the case of a first marriage of a child in his or her twenties, both Jewish and non-Jewish parents sometimes expressed concerns or objections before the marriage. In some cases, Jewish parental pressure during the dating years resulted in a more definitively Jewish character for the eventual household. In other cases, however, the non-Jewish spouses were thoroughly alienated by Jewish pressure. In households that had always directly discouraged marriage outside the faith, after mixed marriage two-thirds of parents continued to express negative feelings, or at least ambivalence, toward the mixed-married household. However, among those who had never commented to their children one way or the other about marriage outside the faith, two-thirds were warmly accepting of the mixed-married couple.

Religiously oriented people are more likely to express concern about marrying across religious lines, to talk about marrying a person of the same faith in a positive vein, and also to express negative feelings about interfaith marriages. The Catholic father of Carlos Martinez, for example, made it clear to his son that he would prefer him not to marry a Jewish woman: "One time when I broke up with Irit, the last time we broke up, I told my Dad about the relationship. And he was actually happy, even though I was in pain, because I wasn't going out with a Jewish girl. And that was the first and last time I ever talked to him about my relationship with a woman. Because he said the Jewish people were the ones that killed Christ." Nevertheless, when Irit and Carlos had reconciled and Carlos told his father that they had decided to marry, his father accepted Irit warmly, according to Carlos, because he saw how much Carlos loved her.

Harsh words uttered by the other side of the family were remembered and quoted many years after the fact, often to illustrate their bigotry. Carol Millstein bitterly recalled her future brother-in-law commenting, "'Well, now I'm going to tell Mom and Dad the bad news.' That was what they thought of me—I'm bad news! It doesn't matter what I am as a person!" Although she now cooperates in raising her converted-into-Judaism children as Jews, she feels no motivation to become Jewish herself.

Many participants came from families in which mixed marriage had already become the family pattern. One Christian wife commented, for example, "Two of my husband's three sisters are married to—well, actually they are both Catholic, their husbands are Catholic. Then he has one other sister who is married to someone who is Jewish. So it's not a burning issue for his family."

It was not unusual for marriage to a non-Jew to be perceived by the Jewish parents as vastly superior to marrying a fervently Orthodox Jew. For example, a young man who had married a woman from a "seriously messed up WASPy family" recalled that his father was traumatized when his sister's Jewish marriage resulted in ultra-Orthodox life in Israel. Consequently, his father was not nearly as upset as he would otherwise have been when the young man brought home his very non-Jewish bride.

Although the proposed mixed marriage sometimes causes short-lived initial discord in one or both families, the arrival of children often melts the hostilities. As a successful businessman who grew up in a "strict" Christian home remembers, at first "my mother was very upset that my children would be Jewish." But once the children actually were born, "they love the children and they love Joyce." His wife's Jewish parents, initially unhappy about her marrying a non-Jew, also relented when the children were born, and "invited me into the family business."

3

THE WEDDING PLANNERS

For couples who marry across ethnic and religious lines, planning the wedding is often the first major challenge of their lives together. For many of them, decisions made during the planning of their weddings become a backdrop for later ethnoreligious negotiations. Although many Americans postpone marriage, when they do decide to marry the details of their marriages are important to them. This was true for both Jewish and non-Jewish spouses in our study. As Joellen recalled:

> Caleb has all along been fairly indifferent to religious practice because he considers himself an atheist, but it was important to me to have some religious content to the wedding. This was as an adult one of my first negative experiences with Judaism. We went around and nobody really wanted to talk about marrying us. We went to Hillel and they would marry us outside the chapel but not in the chapel. And the temple wouldn't have us, and then we couldn't get a rabbi. So finally we got a rabbi's son to marry us as a Justice of the Peace in our backyard.

American popular culture presents Jewish families as preoccupied with marriage, and this perception is strongly linked to historical fact. The blessings recited at each Jewish life cycle event underscore the prominence of marriage in Jewish societies. For centuries in traditional communities governed by rabbinic guidelines, marriage was a strong desideratum, encouraged by both religious dictates and social pressure. Jewish religion and social culture have not been especially tolerant of unmarried adults until relatively recently, and traditional Jewish texts presented the married household as the only productive status for Jewish men and women. Significantly, while children were regarded as one important goal of marriage, the creation of a companionate, Jewishly functioning household equaled fertility as a cultural ideal. Fertility was important not only for its own sake but because it comprised the first step in the task of raising children so that they too would grow up to marry another Jew and create their own "faithful household in Israel," to quote the traditional Jewish wedding language. As marriages were consecrated by the recitation of special blessings and the reading of the *ketubah,* the Jewish marriage contract, under the *huppah,* the wedding canopy, "from generation to generation" was not an abstract concept but a concrete formula for familial and communal functioning.

For many contemporary American Jews, weddings with a traditional Jewish flavor are very desirable. The current attractiveness of Jewish marriage customs represents a reversal of previous trends. In America during the first half of the twentieth century, traditional Jewish wedding customs were familiar only to Jews and were not uniformly popular even in the Jewish community. Acculturated Jews often discarded traditional Jewish wedding behaviors in favor of Western wedding mores. American Jews, like their Christian neighbors, incorporated legions of bridesmaids in matching dresses and often preferred wedding melodies by Mendelssohn and Wagner to anything from Jewish culture.

Within the past few decades, in contrast, Jewish music and foods have been part of the wider American cultural heritage. Americans have become familiarized with lively klezmer wedding music. Jewish wedding dancing and foods are commonplace images in popular commercial films such as *Goodbye, Columbus* and *Private Benjamin* and in numerous television programs. Ironically, while Jewish spouses are sometimes portrayed with negative stereotypes in popular culture (see chapter 8), Jewish weddings are often depicted as lively, warm, and colorful. Having a wedding with a pronounced Jewish flavor is perceived as appealing and not in the least inimical to being an acculturated American.

Being married under a *huppah,* reciting Hebrew blessings, breaking a glass, and calling out "mazel tov" were described by large numbers of our informants as ritualized moments that they wished to incorporate into their own marriage ceremonies. Mixed marrieds, like other American Jews, are apparently very influenced by the Jewish social and cultural emphasis on the sacralization of marriage. It mattered to many of them—or perhaps to their families—that clergy participate in their marriage ceremonies.

Mixed-married couples often went to considerable effort to locate Jewish clergy who were willing to perform or participate in the performance of their wedding ceremonies. In the process, they learned about what considerations went into rabbinic decisions whether or not to perform mixed marriages, as illustrated in the following saga:

> And then by word of mouth, and I forget how we found, but there are two rabbis in the United States that will do a marriage, a Jewish marriage ceremony including the forbidden sentence, which is "according to the laws of Moses and Israel," which is the bit that the rabbi would leave out if it was an interfaith marriage. But we found two of them. We found one and he's a wild guy. He's a hippy. He lives in Malibu. He does his annual High Holidays. And he is the funniest guy. And he said, "Yep."

> **INT:** So he would do a totally Jewish ceremony even though she wasn't Jewish?

> Right. He said are you going to have Jewish children, are you going to raise them Jewish? We said yes. He said are you going to live a Jewish life? We said yes. He said fine. So he married us. We went to California for our wedding and had a wonderful wedding with all the trimmings. My parents were still alive. They came. My wife's grandmother came from England. It was good. It was the last big hurrah for our family. It was the last good portrait of my family. And it was great.

Several informants talked about rabbis who had counseled them as well as performed the ceremony. Sometimes the advice given by these rabbis held the door open for dual religion households:

> We got married in their greenhouse and we had a justice of the peace who really would have done better as a used car salesman. But he did most of the officiating. But we found a Reformed [sic] rabbi who was willing to come and participate in a way that he felt comfortable with. We had gone around to a lot of rabbis who said a) we're not going to marry you, and b) we're not even coming.

> We found a Reformed rabbi who was really great. And we met with him a couple times beforehand. So, we said, "We're going to have to get a third reli-

gion, right, because I can't still keep mine, and she can't keep her religion?"
And he said, "No, you can keep her religion or your religion or keep both of
them, but you don't really need a third religion." And I thought he was actually
pretty smart.

For other couples, it was the priest who located the rabbi to participate in a
dual-clergy ceremony. No matter who found whom, however, the couple
faced the task of negotiating with each other and with their clergymen about
which customs would and wouldn't be made part of the ceremony, and which
ritual utterances would and wouldn't be included.

For Carlos and Irit Martinez, these wedding negotiations were both a re-
flection and a symbol of their linking their lives together. As Carlos remembers,

> We basically said to each other, if we want to be together, we either have it
> all or nothing. But we still wanted to be together. So we decided to go and share
> all the experiences, Catholic and Jewish. . . . What separates a lot of couples is
> their parents' and grandparents' and great-grandparents' pain.
>
> I personally have gone through a transformation of my own of freeing myself
> up of all these things. It has taken a long time, but ever since I did my whole life
> has got into a freight train with no brakes. There are no limits, there's no box. . . .
>
> We had a rabbi and a priest, and it was held in a really nice hotel in the city.
> We prepared the ceremony, we had chosen passages from the Bible, but they
> [the clergymen] just decided to do their own thing at the end. I have to say it
> was definitely tilted toward the Jewish side, because at the end there was no
> mention of anything with the New Testament. It was just very Old Testament,
> and then it even had an Apache blessing, which is beautiful.

Not uncommonly, informants talked about having two separate wedding
ceremonies in two different religions. In most of these cases, Jewish families
attended both ceremonies:

We had two ceremonies. We had a church ceremony and then we had a traditional Jewish ceremony.

INT: Who conducted the church ceremony?

A priest. It was in a church.

INT: And what was that like?

It was beautiful. And due to the curiosity of my family and her family the place was packed. We had five hundred people there.

INT: Due to curiosity?

I would say so. The Jews to go to church and see a wedding.

INT: And the second ceremony?

Was in the reception hall.

INT: And that you said was Jewish? Who conducted that?

A rabbi. An interfaith rabbi did marriages there.

INT: What was that wedding like?

That was a traditional Jewish wedding with prayers and breaking the glass. And prayers. Wine. Very traditional. We had skull caps.

INT: And how many people attended that one?

Three hundred people that went to the reception.

INT: Was this the same day?

Yes, but two ceremonies.

Sometimes one or the other families had negative feelings about the match. These feelings were often expressed in response to wedding arrangements:

It was conducted by a Reform rabbi in the restaurant underneath an archway so we could call it a chuppah. So we had a civil ceremony first. Her mother wanted a Catholic wedding, even though she wasn't really Catholic. I didn't really like the idea, but I went along with it. I think they worked really hard, and Clara got really stressed on making this whole big wedding for her mother. And as Clara tells it, her mother cried the whole time and really was a burden on Clara and wasn't very helpful. So I went back, did the civil ceremony. A day or two later, I had the religious ceremony.

For those informants who wanted some type of religious auspices for their wedding, some eventually "settled for" a minister, rather than not having any religious character at all:

> I don't think there were people in Denver who married interfaith. Or rabbis in Denver that married interfaith. And we searched around and we found a licensed minister or whatever who could perform weddings in the state of Colorado. And, interestingly enough, he had gone through the same thing himself like seven, eight years prior to that . . . he was Jewish and his wife wasn't. And he couldn't find anyone to marry them.

A substantial proportion of mixed married couples either do not want a religious ceremony or turn by default to a judge or justice of the peace, or to some other non-sectarian officiant or friend: "I clerked for a judge in Colorado and he was also a guy that knew Christine's dad and a guy that I still consider him a friend and he presided over our wedding. So, he's like an African-American judge presiding over, you know, a wedding of a Jew and a non-Jew. It was a pretty informal wedding ceremony."

Exogamy, Endogamy, and Marital Stability

Given the special tensions that negotiating two religious traditions bring to a relationship—amply evident in the narratives in this book—what do statistics reveal about the demographic prognosis for mixed-married families with children? According to the American Religious Identification Survey 2001 (ARIS), conducted by researchers from the Graduate Center of City University of New York, interfaith households are three times more likely to end in divorce as families in which both parents share the same faith. ARIS data reinforce the earlier findings of the 1990 NJPS that Jewish mixed-married households are twice as likely to end in divorce as Jewish inmarried households.

These ARIS data examining marital stability and mixed marriage in the various Christian denominations and Islam, as well as among Jewish respondents, are very significant for several reasons. First, by demonstrating that all American mixed marriage, even between two Christian denominations, is far more likely to end in divorce than inmarriage, the ARIS study demonstrates the association of marital stability with endogamy. For years, parents of mixed-married couples have accused Jewish communal leaders who articulate a principled preference for endogamy of contributing to the marital friction of mixed-married households through their intransigence and insensitivity. The ARIS data, however, suggest that religious differences themselves contribute to greater spousal tensions. Marital problems within mixed marriage probably arise primarily from internal—rather than external—sources.

Second, the ARIS data dramatically illustrate the fact that the more demanding wings of Christianity, especially Catholicism and Pentecostalism, are the big "winners" in mixed-married households, in terms of children being raised in the same faith as their parents. According to both the 1990 NJPS and the 2000 NJPS, far fewer than half of the children in mixed-married households with one Jewish parent are described by their parents as "raised Jewish." The ARIS data looks at diverse types of interfaith households nationally. Among families with one Catholic parent, two-thirds (66 percent) are raising their children as Catholics. Among families with one Pentecostal parent, 65 percent of children are raised as Pentecostalists. Among families with one Baptist or Presbyterian parent, 63 percent each are raised as Baptists or Presbyterians. Among the Christian denominations, only Episcopalianism and Anglicanism at 39 percent each approach Judaism's low holding power.

It is significant that many "mainstream" religious groups that have more difficulty in retaining the interest of their young people, such as Episcopalian and Protestant wings of American Christianity, share with American Judaism a profile of political liberalism, ideological tolerance, and inclusivity—and few religious boundaries and demands![3]

Divorce has important connections to mixed marriage. Mixed marriages are twice as likely to break up in divorce as inmarriages, according to 1990 NJPS data. And about twice as many Jews marry non-Jews the "second time around." Like Woody Allen's character Alvy Singer in *Annie Hall* (1978), many participants described one or more relationships or marriages to a Jewish but otherwise dramatically unsuitable person before their successful relationships or marriages to non-Jews. Guy Naiman chose Jewish-but-irretrievably-flawed spouses twice before his currently happy marriage to a Christian woman. Naiman bitterly remembers the socioeconomic pressure he experienced during a brief marriage to his first Jewish wife:

> My first wife was an extremely wealthy heiress and I was married to her for about a minute and a half. Even that was too long!

Actually, we were married about nine months and she gave birth and was gone. . . .

I was a struggling, very struggling young man. I got married at the age of twenty-five. I was trying to go out there and make my way and she wanted me to take certain things from her family. I said I was brought up a certain way, with a certain idea of how you behave and how you get the things you want in life. You earn them.

Her family wanted me to move to a certain home and I looked at this house and I said, "You're twenty-three. I'm twenty-five. Who is going to clean this house? I can't even afford a maid, much less pay for the house." Her parents said, "We'll take care of it." I said, "I'm not interested." And then they gave me a check. I looked at it and I said, "What is this?" Her father said, "It's a down payment on the house." I said, "I told you, we're not moving into this house." He said, "You're taking the check." I said, "I'm not taking the check because I wouldn't take this check from my own father. My own father wouldn't give it to me. He would say, go earn it." Her father repeated, "You're keeping it." . . .

There was this struggle, and I finally said, "We can do with this as we please?" He said, "Absolutely." So I took the check and ripped it up! Then I called, "Sheila," and we walked out. And this is a very famous family. And we walked out. We went home.

The next day, Sheila called me at work, and she said, "I'm home." I said, "Well, that's where you're supposed to be." She said, "No, I'm home with my parents. And I'm not coming back." I said, "What are you talking about?" She said, "I'm not in love. I'm getting a divorce."

Naiman said he fought the divorce for a year and a half but couldn't match the clout of his father-in-law's money. "They flew her off," he said, and he lost touch with his son for eighteen years. Eventually, however, he reestablished a relationship with the boy, and he now sees him frequently.

Guy Naiman's marriages to two Jewish women were short-lived, and then he married his present wife, Carla Chambord, who retains her name. Part of what turned Naiman off to Judaism was the manipulativeness of his Jewish wives and their families. However, Naiman's ambivalence about Judaism predated his unfortunate marital experiences, as we saw earlier. He himself traces his apathy about Jewishness back to the fact that the home he grew up in provided him with little in the way of substantive Jewish education, either formal or informal. Their minimal religious life, by his account, was a matter of going through certain rituals, with little emphasis on their meaning or relevance.

The process of planning a wedding was frequently described as a climactic event. Wedding planning occupied a great deal of time and energy. It often seemed at the time an implementation of decisions that the couple thought they had already made about the ethnoreligious character of their households—or lack thereof. However, later these couples began to perceive their weddings as providing not so much closure and stability as a portal into the process of new negotiations. Through subsequent years, many of our informants discovered that the enterprise of creating a custom-made household that reflected both of their evolving thoughts and feelings was not a closed chapter but a continuing conversation.

4

INVENTING NEW SELVES AND TRADITIONS

Until relatively recently most people were born into ethnoreligious societies and became identified with those groups. In twenty-first-century America, however, large segments of the population are arguably freer than ever before to "invent" themselves as individuals. Within the broad spectrum of "white" Americans, individuals can choose to identify with one or another ethnic group or religion, or to create hybrid new models combining aspects of two or more traditions.[4] For the Ben-David-Martinez family, as we have seen, this meant incorporating an Apache blessing into an otherwise "Jewish-leaning" wedding ceremony. Often an eclectic or syncretic style of ethnoreligious invention emerges as an aspect of interfaith interpersonal relationships.

One might reasonably expect most mixed-married families to simply abandon the idea of ethnoreligious identity altogether, and indeed some do. However, most retain at least some religious observances and identity. Observers from outside the United States are often mystified at the resiliency of the impulse to identify religiously among Americans. In diverse European countries, highly educated persons frequently reject religion and ethnicity as concepts that are outmoded and/or unnecessarily divide people into antagonistic groups. Israel also is home to a prominent population of committed secularists. However, Americans, as poll after poll shows, are somewhat different: for most of them, religion and ethnicity are important building blocks as they style their personal and household identities. True secularism—that is, principled nontheism—is not nearly as prevalent in the United States as it is in many other international settings. Enthusiasm for religious and/or cultural identification stems partially from a stubborn American cultural bias toward religiosity, coupled with a social ethos that since the 1960s has increasingly embraced multiculturalism and ethnic particularism, with accompanying religious diversity.[5]

Herbert Gans and other observers of American Jewish life have argued that the current flowering of interest in ethnic and religious particularism is only skin deep, a kind of "symbolic ethnicity" that does not much affect daily life.[6] While this may be true, ethnic and religious choices are very compelling to many Americans, even those who choose to combine traditions. For most of this study's interview participants, the enterprise of wrestling with differing traditions was a deep and ongoing aspect of their adult family lives.

Interestingly, freedom of choice in multicultural America has made life easier for people who identify actively with one religious group. Americans identifying with one particular religious tradition, even a minority religion such as Judaism, today face less social stigma and fewer negative educational, occupational, or economic consequences than ever before. Rewards for abandoning cultural distinctiveness have declined dramatically along with the homogenizing ethos of the melting pot that held sway at the turn of the twentieth century. American warmth toward ethnoreligious diversity has given rise to scholarly, artistic, and popular materials that explore and celebrate minority cultures. Indeed, for a substantial segment of the American Jewish community, a veritable cultural renaissance has been developing for nearly half a century.

Thus, very few interview participants said that they chose not to identify themselves as Jews because they suffered from bigotry at some point in their lives. While most informants voiced the idea that "being Jewish makes you different," few had taken the option of "passing" as a member of some other ethnic or religious group. Most chose instead the strategy of revealing their Jewish identity selectively. In other words, they personally identified as Jews but only told those people they felt would not discriminate against them because of their Jewishness. Although it might seem as though being "nothing" would be an attractive option, most American Jews who do not feel "religious" choose to identify at least as "cultural" or "secular" Jews, rather as no ethnic group at all.

Americans are free to select one ethnic or religious heritage and to immerse themselves as deeply or as shallowly as they wish in its waters. They can also opt for combining a number of ethnic and/or religious traditions, and for selecting for their families a double or hybrid religious heritage—or none at all. Men and women who marry across what used to be fairly firm boundaries of peoplehood and/or faith often create new combinations of ethnic and religious behaviors, and merged or syncretic traditions—what Mary Waters calls "ethnic options."[7] Selecting personalized options further extends a sociological "pattern of mixing" that has long been one of the defining characteristics of American life.[8]

Perhaps because ethnic and religious identification plays such an important role in American culture, my study revealed that the majority of mixed-married couples started talking about the possible religious character of their potential households while they were dating, with their first realization that the relationship had become serious. This discovery was something of a surprise, because background literature about mixed-married couples, primarily drawn from the experiences of workshop leaders and outreach workers, argues that many couples do not begin to wrestle with complicated issues around the religious/ethnic nature of the household until they are contemplating a family. We began the interviewing process with the hypothesis that we too would find this pattern. However, the majority of both Jewish and Christian informants in this study recalled that family faith issues were discussed while dating, and this was true both of first and second marriage situations. One Jewish partner described the premarital negotiating process:

> Well, it was never about my religion versus his religion. It was more conversation about—you have to understand this is both of our second marriages, and the whole point of us, if we are even thinking about getting married, is that we are not going to make the same mistake twice. So we need to get everything on the table and then work backwards. So the biggest controversy, obviously, was how would we bring up the children. It wasn't a controversy, but it was a conversation. That's how we got started.

The partner with the strongest religious background and/or beliefs usually wanted the children to be raised in his or her faith. However, frequently Jewish spouses wanted their children to be raised as Jews even when they did not have particularly extensive knowledge of Judaism and/or patterns of religious involvement. In those cases, the more religiously involved Christian partner insisted that the Jewish partner upgrade his or her involvement with Judaism if the family religion was going to be Judaism.

In other words, although the determination that the household religion would be Jewish came from the Jew, the insistence that the household would have a more intensive involvement with religion came from a non-Jewish parent who was concerned that the children should have a full and rich religious life:

> My philosophy is I only know one religion, and if I am going to be their mother, I can only bring them up Jewish. Plus in fact I don't believe in Catholicism. So if I believed a little bit in Catholicism, I would think about it. But there is just—you don't do that. So he was actually very good about it. I mean, I don't know. I have been very lucky. It wasn't that he didn't challenge me, but his response was, "I'll tell you what—I have no problem with you bringing the children up Jewish. However, that means bring them up Jewish. Don't just say they are Jewish. I want them in Hebrew School, I want bar and bat mitzvahs. I want them to be married in a temple. I want them to understand the Jewish culture. And if you can hold up to that end of the bargain, then great."

Although many of the Jewish informants remembered that as teenagers and college students they felt Judaism was not particularly important, when faced with the possibility of creating a primarily non-Jewish household, they found—often to their surprise—that their Jewishness was more central to their identities than they had imagined. Like Yonina Ben David-Moumad below, the Jewish partner often issued an ultimatum, declaring at some point prior to marriage that he or she would not marry the non-Jewish partner unless the children were raised as Jews.

> Then, I said, "Look. If we're going to think about this, we need to take some steps." And, this thing evolved and we thought this through very early on, because there was no opportunity for compromise as far as I was concerned. I wasn't going to have kids with a Jewish and Moslem kind of thing. I don't think that works. It might work for some people, but I just kind of see religion as you've got to pick one and if you're called to the Torah, you're called to the Torah as a Jew—not as a Jew and something else. Maybe you could do a Jew and a Buddhist. I don't know that much about it.

Most informants said this discussion took place well before marriage. Both Jewish men and Jewish women said they initiated such discussions while dating. As one non-Jewish father of two Jewish toddlers remembered, after meeting his wife in a beach house in West Hampton and dating her "off and on for about four years," the two of them felt the relationship getting "serious." "We started to discuss religion. She said the kids had to be Jewish." Many non-Jewish spouses said they saw from their first discussions that no marriage would take place unless there was a clear verbal commitment to raising the children as Jews: "She felt so strongly—I knew I had to compromise, because that was the way it was going to be."

Having discovered that religious identity was one of the first compelling issues in their lives together, many couples described the process of determining in which religion they could comfortably raise their children. Their discussions were lengthy, requiring patience, research, experimentation, and thoughtfulness on both sides. Sometimes the non-Jewish partner needed to re-evaluate Christianity to determine how much it mattered, such as the woman who reflected, "I really wanted Chad to find out for sure whether or not he had any ties to Catholicism. And, in fact, he didn't. Which I kind of knew, but I think he needed to find out for sure."

The fact that Judaism is the wellspring of Christianity was important for some informants, especially those with some Jewish or Christian textual background. Because Judaism and the Hebrew Bible were among the sources for early Christianity, some Christian spouses felt that they were not really abandoning their own religious traditions when they raised Jewish children. One Jewish wife spoke about her husband:

> Well, actually, it was Cary who said, "You know the Old Testament is part of my religion, and the New Testament is part of my religion but not part of yours," and he said, so I would feel, we both agreed that we couldn't raise them Jewish and Catholic. I read a book called *Mixed Blessings* and that was enough for me. You give a kid one religion, not both, and he was the one who actually said, "I don't feel very uncomfortable raising them Jewish." He said he wouldn't feel uncomfortable with Judaism because it really is part of Catholicism and the Old Testament. And he said that there would not be a whole lot that would make him uncomfortable, but I told him everything about Catholicism would make me uncomfortable. So that was discussed. And he has stuck to that completely because we are raising him Jewish.

In other families, it was not until children were born that the issue of the religion of the household was discussed. Most often, the spouse who didn't feel strongly about his or her religion had the fewest mixed feelings about seeing children raised in another faith—at least when couples discussed their children's faith in the abstract. As we will explore more fully in part II, decisions about how children should be raised frequently underwent revisions later on, when parents felt differently about the decision as they observed their children celebrating holidays that they themselves did not celebrate, and learning languages and prayers that they did not utilize.

Such spouses were often surprised by the strength of their own feelings. Informants described being overwhelmed by emotions, in conversations that sometimes took place before and sometimes after children were born. The realization that they really cared about how their children were raised came as a revelation to them:

> I always kind of told myself it wasn't an important thing. But then we got married and talked about having children, and I suddenly realized that it was important to me, which I know happens to a lot of people. And we had what could have been a dilemma, an obvious dilemma. But we talked about it, and she is not religious at all. And we both agreed that the children should have a religious identity and we decided to raise them to be Jewish.

Other couples studied both religions and what raising children in those religions might feel like. Some went so far as to audition clergy about their decision:

> But as far as religion goes, we actually interviewed rabbis and priests for ourselves. We came to the conclusion that we would most likely be bringing the child up Catholic.
>
> **INT:** And how did you make that decision?
>
> We made it because my wife is more actively Catholic than I am actively Jewish. It doesn't matter to either of us which way as long as there is a definite path. That is basically the way I see it.

Jews and non-Jews who marry each other often begin by being fascinated by the differences in their partner's backgrounds, which at first seem exotic and intriguing. Many feel that they have walked "through the looking glass," in several ways. Being married to someone with a different religious background often has the paradoxical effect of making one feel more intensely aware of the social, cultural, and religious characteristics of one's own background: "I never felt so Jewish until I married my Christian wife." Jewish and non-Jewish spouses often provide and define identification boundaries for each other, in an American society in which external boundaries have become exceedingly porous.

This sense of boundaried difference is often balanced by an exquisite sensitivity to the feelings of one's husband or wife, who embodies the "other." In mixed marriages that work—as in inmarriages that work—spouses care about the impact of their words and actions. Spousal concern about being fair and not obliterating the ethnoreligious heritage of the other is another way in which mixed-married spouses have walked "through the looking glass." Identity politics are tempered by anxiety about hurting the person they love.

Thus, marriages between people of diverging ethnoreligious traditions can make the two spouses more conscious of their own heritages and more knowledgeable and sensitive toward those of other faiths and backgrounds. However, living out dual expectations in the sequence of daily, yearly, and life-cycle decisions is often difficult. And, as we shall see, the impact of doubleness on children is frequently unexpected and hard to predict.

II

LIVING MIXED TRADITIONS

5

DREAMING OF A WHITE—WHATEVER

"I'm dreaming of a white Christmas, just like the ones I used to know," wrote composer Irving Berlin, who emigrated from Russia to the Lower East Side of New York in 1893. "White Christmas," crooned by Bing Crosby in the 1942 film *Holiday Inn,* won the composer an Oscar. It was sung by a broad array of artists over the years and eventually sold forty million records.[1] This tour de force was followed by Berlin's lilting homage to the "Easter Parade," the title song of a 1948 film with Judy Garland that won an Oscar for musical scoring. Berlin wrote 1500 songs, serenading virtually every American holiday and including the patriotic anthem "God Bless America."

Berlin's biographers note that despite his warm memories of music in the synagogue, Berlin married a Christian woman and "didn't see the point of remaining Jewish, as that condition provoked unwarranted persecution."[2] The phenomenon of Jewish musicians, writers, and filmmakers articulating the holiday spirit of Christian America has seemed to some observers symbolic of the inexorable sweep of assimilation. As Jews have triumphantly overcome the boundaries of the geographical, vocational, and socioeconomic ghettos that once circumscribed their lives, profound aspects of Jewish distinctiveness have disappeared.[3] In the words of the assimilationist sociologist Louis Wirth, as Jews become more and more seamlessly incorporated into the fabric of American life, "the ghetto world shrinks to a vanishing point."[4]

Confounding assimilationist expectations, however, Jewish distinctiveness— like that of other ethnic and religious groups—has not actually disappeared in the United States. The resilience of ethnic appeal over the decades came as a surprise to some assimilationists. Although some sociologists persisted in expecting ethnic differences to fade away, by the 1970s others argued that ethnicity seemed to be "unmeltable."[5] Nevertheless, although Jewish distinctiveness is apparent today in many guises, it has undergone complex transformations.[6] Contemporary American Jewish societies and cultures comprise a complicated hybrid, coalescing American values and behaviors with historical Jewish laws, customs, and attitudes.[7] In today's America, it is difficult to describe the "norm" and what constitutes a departure from it. Put simply, it seems harder to say what is "Jewish" and what is not.

Several demographic trends contribute to the blurred definitions of American Jewishness. First, American Jews have established a number of recognized religious movements, each with its own continuum of norms. These American Judaisms diverge from one another in numerous particulars, so that standards central to one wing of Judaism are minimally salient to another.[8] Adding to this Jewish multiculturalism, the sociological influence of immigrant generations diminishes with every passing decade. The increasingly predominant fourth and fifth generations are measurably more Americanized in many ways. Moreover, geographical location also has a homogenizing effect, as a substantial proportion of American Jews emigrates away from the ethnically Jewish flavors of New York and its environs to southern and western sunbelt communities. American Jews often live far from family and childhoods friends, as dramatically illustrated by the 1990 and 2000–2001 National Jewish Population Surveys. Their long-term independence contributes to their sense of freedom and openness, and their ability to create lifestyles for themselves according to their own preferences.[9]

Against this background of diversity and choice, most American Jews experiment with different levels and styles of religious affiliation and practice during their single years. For those who marry, the early years of marriage often become a forum for juggling the traditions of the two families of origin, even when both partners are Jewish. Mixed-married couples face even broader choices as they negotiate holidays and life-cycle events.

Despite personal religious experimentation and Berlin's joyous odes to Christian holidays, however, the observance or non-observance of Christian holidays, and the incorporation—or not—of Christian customs into life-cycle events remains one of the great differences between Jewish- and Christian-affiliated homes. Our interview and focus group participants used the holidays and their life-cycle events as benchmarks for describing their familial religious orientations.

Those families that had decided to raise children as both Christian and Jewish worked conscientiously at doubleness, carefully including both religions' holidays in their calendar year. Those who had decided to raise the children as Jews, however, often struggled to determine whether, and how much, Christian holiday observance would be appropriate in their households, supplementing their Judaic observances. They candidly discussed their struggles and negotiations around the subject of holidays and life-cycle events, and they made it clear that rituals and customs associated with both still have enormous symbolic significance.

When American families are asked what their religious identification means to them, most talk about ceremonial and celebratory moments. The ongoing sequence of quotidian decisions shapes the ethnic and religious culture of each household. As Mary Waters notes, there is currently a strong conservative trend among many ethnic Americans, who are "very interested in keeping the customs alive" even though they often "don't really know what they are for." Studying Roman Catholics from various ethnic backgrounds, Waters found that even when the "significance of the symbols" that are invoked "is almost completely lost," many American ethnics will "try to maintain the actions at least." Perhaps most significant, Waters found that some ethnic Americans enjoy feeling distinctive—at least on ceremonial occasions—and will expend considerable energy maintaining holiday traditions that reflect their ethnic distinctiveness:

> Those respondents who did take part in special ethnic activities on American holidays, or who observed a traditional holiday celebration that most Americans do not follow, clearly enjoyed this aspect of their ethnicity. Such activities are clearly voluntary and intermittent, but it is also clear that they bring pleasure and are relatively easy to do. People enjoy observing special holidays or observing ordinary holidays in a special way, and they like thinking that their families have distinctive traditions.[10]

Life-cycle events such as the births of children or the deaths of loved ones, and the holiday calendar of events including the Jewish "High Holidays," the Christmas season, and New Age or traditional Passover seders, are most frequently mentioned as meaningful frameworks for ethnic or religious ritual and cultural or spiritual expression. Couples grapple first with divergent backgrounds when they plan their weddings. After the wedding, previously abstract ethnic, cultural, and religious decisions are made graphic and concrete in each family's life-cycle ceremonies and holidays.

In the words of Shawn Moskowitz, a teenage focus group participant, "Christmas and Hanukkah are when all of my parents' talk about whether we have a double or a single religion in our household gets real."

Holidays and life-cycle ceremonies are often delightful times, and parents and teenagers have warm comments about many aspects of their family celebrations. However, studies repeatedly show—and my interview and focus group participants spelled it out in detail—that special events are fraught with dissonant expectations and anxieties for many people. This is true even when spouses share a religious heritage, or when a family has no religion. Holidays and ceremonial occasions tend to magnify tensions. Even seemingly benign, nonsectarian occasions such as Thanksgiving dinners are notorious settings for family blow-ups.

These occasions often bring together family members at various transition points. In the spotlight of public settings, as well as a heightened family awareness, sensitivities about changes in life-cycle status can be exacerbated. Extended families and the divergent friendship groups of different family members also add to the sometimes volatile mix of dramatically differing expectations.

When these already complex family equations are further complicated by differing religious traditions, the implications of decision-making and the potential for familial tension often increase exponentially. Some of these tensions have become part of the American vocabulary: newspapers and magazines regularly devote articles to the "December dilemma," referring to the increasingly prominent proportion of mixed-married American households that struggle to decide how much attention to pay to Christmas and/or Hanukkah.

Family stories about these cycles of celebration provide an easily accessible focal point for Jewish and non-Jewish spouses to analyze the place of religion and ethnicity in their lives. Our study participants talked about familial evolutions, describing the ways in which celebrations of religious holidays and life-cycle events change over the years; which aspects of religious or ethnic activities really touch people, and which leave them cold; how grandparents, aunts, uncles, cousins, and other extended family members interact in these cycles of celebration; and how their families are influenced by the broader cultural milieu. Looking at what people say about holiday celebrations and life-cycle event ceremonies provides us with not only a window into behaviors and attitudes, but also a "through the looking-glass" vision of how various family members interpret and reinterpret family decisions and activities.

Negotiating Two Traditions

The freedom to compose eclectic holiday styles feels liberating to some couples. At the same time, these open options often generate anxiety, because they differ from the experiences of the two spouses in their families of origin. Most Jews do not celebrate Christmas or Easter festivities in their homes. Christian symbols are found in a mere 2 percent of homes of American Jews who are members of a synagogue. The overall figures, according to the 2000–01 National Jewish Population Study, indicate that only 6 percent of American Jews report they always or usually have a Christmas tree.[11] Conversely, the celebration of Jewish festivals, with their accompanying Hebrew prayers and blessings, is rare in Christian homes, with the exception of Passover seder meals, which are becoming popular in some churches and other locations.

However, in mixed-married households, in dramatic contrast, the intermingling of Jewish and Christian holidays is one of the most prevalent patterns. Mixed-married spouses often see this as a way of being fair to both spouses, their families, and their faith traditions. Most mixed-married families report some connection to both Christmas and Hanukkah, Passover and Easter. Sixty percent of mixed-married families that identify as Jewish by religion have a Christmas tree in their homes.

How these dual connections are handled depends partially on the way the household has designed its religious identity. For those couples that have decided to raise their children with double ethnoreligious orientations, marking both Jewish and Christian holidays is a matter of principle. Celebrating both Hanukkah and Christmas, Passover and Easter, is the way self-described dual-faith families show themselves and the world that they are raising children with two heritages. This is also the group most likely to include attendance at church services as part of their holiday festivities. Typically, those couples who say they are raising their children with two religions try to provide their children with a verbal context that encompasses both: "We talk about his being Jewish. And we also talk about having a Presbyterian background."

Crystalle and Gary Moskat, a Colorado couple who joined the local Jewish Community Center for their outstanding toddlers' child care, talked about their family's "fair" and "balanced" celebration of Christian and Jewish spring holidays. Gary, the Jewish father, described their family festivals:

> Easter we have bagels and lox and the kids hunt for eggs. It's a non-religious kind of a chocolate fest, that sort of a thing.
>
> Then Passover, we have friends, a different couple where the wife is Jewish, the husband is not. And we celebrate with them and they have a good friend of theirs who I've become friends with through them and she is Jewish. And so she comes with her boyfriend who is Jewish also. And then we try to invite one non-Jewish couple to kind of expose them to the Passover seder. They're not real super religious either. So we have a rather abbreviated ceremony partly because of kids, partly because she's just not into doing the whole Haggadah thing. So we celebrate that.
>
> Then I guess we don't do anything for Rosh Hashanah or Yom Kippur. We used to. We lived in Wisconsin, again, we sort of had these friends where one was Jewish, one wasn't, that we'd hook up with for Passover. And then we would hook up usually for Rosh Hashanah, Yom Kippur, but not to Temple.

However, it is not only families raising their children in two faiths who incorporate Christian observances into their family life. Most mixed-married couples who describe themselves as "raising all our children as Jews" also report incorporating Christian holiday festivities into their calendars. However, they are much less likely to attend church services and much more likely to describe struggling with holiday decisions or to speak in ways that reinterpret Christian activities semantically as being "cultural" or "nonreligious" rather than "religious."

Joellen and Caleb Masterson decided early in their marriage to celebrate both sets of holidays as they raise their "Jewish" children:

> They are being raised Jewish, but you know Caleb's family are seriously practicing Christians and we made a decision early on that we would celebrate Christmas. There is also an acknowledgement of Easter, but none of them have religious content. They have cultural content. We do it that way because I

didn't want to force Caleb's family into sending Hanukkah presents one day and the next day celebrate Christmas.

Joellen cites her Jewishness as the reason she is so sensitive about Caleb's family's feelings: "My concern about them stems from my own experience at being left out of the Christian seasonal festivals."

Chad Markquardt, the Christian husband of a couple who reported themselves as raising Jewish children, also described the incorporation of Christian activities into their family life. He talked about looking forward to reading to his daughters about Jesus in the manger on Christmas Eve, calling this activity "just cultural."

The American ideal of sharing, compromising, and blending is an important consideration for many couples as they plan family holidays. Conflict between two ethnoreligious traditions can catch family members by surprise. Some feel unhappy that putatively joyous occasions have become the focal point for conflict. Under these circumstances, one strategy is to abandon or adapt religious activities that trouble one spouse. Another very common strategy is to reinterpret one religious tradition—usually Christianity—as not being really a religion but rather a kind of cultural enrichment.

As we have seen, Jewish father Gary Moskat used this strategy when he referred to his family's Easter celebrations as a "chocolate fest" but described their admittedly "abbreviated" Passover seders with more seriousness. Christian father Chad Markquardt called reading from the New Testament "just cultural" and then continued with some interesting reflections on what made a given activity "religious" or "cultural." According to Markquardt, holiday observances done in the name of a minority religion implied difference—sectarianism—and were thus by definition "religious." In contrast, holiday observances done as part of the majority religion, because they had already permeated the culture, were not sectarian and could therefore be described as cultural, no matter how steeped they were in religious significance. Thus, he could refer to reading about baby Jesus on Christmas eve as a cultural activity because it is part of the majority culture, whereas reading from the Haggadah at the Passover seder was to him clearly religious because it refers to the Jews:

> I have kind of had my qualms about how far to go . . . there is an asymmetry generally, I think, of the minority religion, and how much of the majority

religious influence it can handle—or rather my wife and her friends can handle. Versus me, a majority religious person, and how much of the minority religion I can handle . . . I think partly it's the sobriety or just the emotional attitude that we take to those different things. Let's take the seder. The seder is much more religious. I mean, it's talking about the Jewish people, and there are very specific things you say. It's not just in the foreign language, which is kind of interesting and different, but it's calling upon you to practice and be a good Jew, and here's what you should remember.

Basically, seder is an extremely religious activity with a lot of good food.

Jewish Reactions to Christian Holiday Activities

Even compromise does not necessarily resolve mixed feelings on the part of mixed-married spouses. The Moskats reported that despite their ecumenical Easter bagels-and-chocolate-eggs concessions, the "December dilemma" emerged early in their marriage as a difficult religious issue. The intensity of their individual feelings surprised them. Crystalle hardly expected her husband Gary to make a scene about Christmas celebrations. Gary was the fourth of four siblings to marry a non-Jew. His parents, according to both Gary and Crystalle, always behaved warmly toward Crystalle, and they generally showed little passion about Judaism, by her account. As a result, she was shocked by the antagonism Gary and his family showed toward the Christmas tree.

> For reasons that I still don't totally understand, Gary is very opposed to a Christmas tree in the house. I mean the fact that there's one at my mother's house, you know, he's okay with that. But he doesn't want a Christmas tree in our house. And actually before we got married, I don't know, I might have just said something in passing about getting a tree or something. And I was shocked that he was so opposed to it. But he was.
>
> And his mother is the same way. I mean they have this thing about the Christmas tree and they don't like it in public places, particularly if they're educational kinds of places. But I think my family would be very disappointed to come for Christmas and there be, like, no—all there would be is that little potted plant over there. I don't think it would be quite the same for them. But other than the tree, it's sort of been the only thing.
>
> And it was more, it turned into a big thing more because I just couldn't figure out what the big deal was about it, but it was a big deal. And I've talked to

other people, you know, I've asked other people. And some of my friends who are Jewish are like, oh, yeah, the tree is out. I mean the tree is a bad thing. So I still haven't figured out why exactly it's so bad, but it is.

Surprisingly negative reactions to the reality of Christmas trees were described by many Jewish spouses, especially those who had determined that they would raise their children as Jews. Janice MacKelroy remembers that Christian observance "didn't bother me much before we were married." It wasn't until she became pregnant at age thirty-eight that she found herself reacting negatively to the observance of Christian holidays. Janice and her husband, Chuck, had decided that they would have Jewish children but expose them to their Christian heritage through Chuck and his family. This decision was fine with Janice as long as they were dating.

As Janice remembers it before marriage she felt fine about celebrating Christmas with Chuck's family: "I said, it's no big deal." However, once they started a family,

it was uncomfortable for me at Christmas and Easter. I always dreaded it. I felt, I've tried and tried, Chuck probably understands this more than anybody and has explained it a zillion times, but I felt I was betraying my religion.

When we'd go and decorate the tree, I'd be, like, should I go and do this? This is something that I couldn't seem to separate, that this is just a family function, it's not, you know, it was like ooooooooooh [groan]. It was uncomfortable, very uncomfortable for me. And I still don't like going over there to decorate the tree with my kids. I have a real problem with it. I can't explain why.

Janice and Chuck MacKelroy's insistence that all Christian activities will be in the homes of grandparents and other extended family members, and that there will be no Christian observances in their own home, places them among the minority of mixed-married couples who decide on, establish, and maintain over the years a primarily Jewish holiday calendar. Chuck described their thinking, their rules, and the way they explain them to the grandparents and the children:

We go to my parent's house for Christmas. This is a real, I guess, delicate situation, because we're concerned—we don't want to give our kids a mixed message. And we really try to reinforce with my parents that we really don't want to give the boys Christmas presents. We want my parents to give them

Hanukkah presents. I mean if I have my family up here for Hanukkah for one of the nights, that's where we want them to give Hanukkah gifts.

Now we go there to celebrate Christmas and my sister, they've got their two kids, that's when they're going to get their presents from my parents. And so my parents have had like a token gift there. They each have a stocking, you know, filled with fruit and candy and a couple little, like, knickknacks, so we do that.

We try to explain to Jamie that we're going over there not to celebrate Christmas but to observe or to respect Grammy and Big Pops's celebration. And I don't know if it sinks in or if they understand it, but we try to get the message across that just because you go, it doesn't mean you believe in it. It's that it's important to Grammy and Big Pops, it's their holiday.

Chuck's words and holiday strategy are virtually identical to those employed by most of the conversionary families we interviewed. "We help Gramma and Grandpa celebrate their holiday. It's not our holiday" was nearly a mantra among conversionary parents. However, the reaction of the families of mixed-married couples was often different from that of the conversionary families. When mixed-married couples tried to create an exclusively Jewish household, Christian extended family members often tried to undermine that resolve. They tended to think of the children as "half and half." As a result, they felt that it was unfair to deprive a half-Christian child of Christian holiday celebrations in his or her own home.

As Chuck put it, "My family can be passive-aggressive at times," attempting to bypass parental decisions by slipping a Christian reminder past the family rules. Several mixed-married couples complained with considerable agitation that Christian extended family members were "breaking the rules" by bringing to their "Jewish homes" deliberately and overtly Christmasy papered gifts, or chocolate bunnies and Easter eggs.

Ruth Ginsburg, the grown child of a conversionary household, remembered that when she went to her grandmother's house for Christmas she received presents marked "From the dog" as a way of striking back at her Jewish mother for not allowing her to get Christmas presents. Christmas and the presents in this case became a weapon for expressing years of hostile feelings:

My grandfather is actually a Methodist minister. So he definitely came from a not-Jewish family.

He hated my mother. I would assume, since they got married because my mother was pregnant—at the time that was what you did—I would assume that he felt that my father was trapped into marrying her and trapped into converting because my mother's family was very, very traditionally Jewish. So he was very bitter about it for a very long time.

Now we would all go there for Christmas, and my cousins would be getting toys from Santa, and I'd be getting gifts from the dog.

Chuck MacKelroy expanded on this theme, saying that his parents "resented" not being able to take their grandchildren to church "and my parents would show off the grandkids, that type of thing."

As a rule, when Christian-raised persons became Jews by choice, their family members respected the holiday house rules, because they did not think of the children in these families as "half Christian." Psychologically, even when the families of converts were unhappy with their decision to convert, they did see their children and their children's children as being Jewish. Under these circumstances they understood why it would be inappropriate to bring Christian symbols into a Jewish home.

For some Jewish spouses, incorporating Christmas into their mixed-married families represented no break with the past, because their parents had already included aspects of Christmas in the homes they grew up in. Josh Mandlebaum, for example, remembered feeling confused by his family's quasi-Christmas celebrations as a child:

> I never really understood why we to a certain extent celebrated Christmas. I guess I must feel like it's a little touchy or I would have brought this up to you before now. I mean we never had a tree, but we had stockings over the mantle. And for a couple of years, my Dad did the thing where you bring out the hot chocolate and the cookie to make it look like Santa Claus came. And we also— one thing I do remember, we opened big gifts on Christmas day. I mean that was, no matter, even if Hanukkah might have come during Christmas, a number of years in the mid- to late sixties we opened up a lot of gifts on Christmas.
>
> So I don't know. I mean I thought maybe it's like an assimilationist kind of thing to make us feel we were, you know, we didn't miss out on those [Christmas] traditions.
>
> But at a certain point it stopped. I guess probably at the same time we were getting a little old to be getting big gifts anyway.

Changes in the American ethos may have been an important influence on the decision about when the inmarried-parent Mandelbaums stopped having Christmas celebrations. Although Josh himself does not make this association, the late 1960s and the early 1970s represent the period when American culture shifted from an espousal of the melting pot to an embrace of multiculturalism, pluralism, and ethnic particularism. The cultural hegemony of white middle-class Christian traditions frayed around the edges, and the proportion of Jewish families who felt it necessary to provide their children with Christmas festivities declined.

Today, relatively few Jewish-Jewish households have Christmas trees or other types of Christian celebrations in their homes, as we have noted. In contrast, Christian observances are reported by all types of mixed-married households: those raising their children with a double religious heritage, Jewish and Christian; those raising them with no religion; and even among most (but not all) of those who say that they are raising their children as Jews. Interestingly, mixed-married Jews who insisted that they had no religion whatsoever in their homes almost universally had Christmas tree and wreaths. What "no religion" means to this group, therefore, is the incorporation of Christian activities that are so widely practiced in the culture that they can be regarded as having no religious significance.

Couples who define their Christian activities as "just cultural" are often deeply convinced that their Christmas trees and Easter egg hunts are entirely secular, and that they may experience them as simply pleasant, "fun" activities. However, as their children grow up experiencing these activities in their own homes, they take psychological ownership of a Christian religious tradition. These festivities, and the religious traditions out of which they grew, belong to the child. When children from double-celebrating mixed-married households get to college, they often define themselves as "half Jews," participating in email conversations and forming campus clubs by this name even when their parents have assumed that they are raising Jewish children. Celebrating Christian festivals—however secular—sends a message to children, and this message is not lost.

Jewish Holiday Activities

Some mixed-married families define themselves as unambiguously Jewish. These families make and maintain a principled decision that their religious activities, including home-based family celebrations as well as religious institutional affiliation and attendance, will be exclusively Jewish. Unambiguously Jewish families go to great lengths to create a clear distinction between their own Jewish orientations and the Christian observances of grandparents and other family members. For example, the Talbots established early on in their marriage that they would visit their Christian inlaws during the Christmas season to show their respect and support for their holiday, but not on the day of Christmas itself, "because we want our children to know that this isn't our holiday—it's Nana's and Poppa's." These families also often ask their Christian relatives not to send Christmas presents or Easter goodies to the house.

Families raising their children exclusively as Jews are far more likely than two-religion or no-religion mixed-married households to report High Holy Day attendance at synagogue or temple. As a symbol of the support the non-Jewish spouse lends to this arrangement, in unambiguously Jewish mixed-married households a majority of non-Jewish spouses attended High Holy Day services with their Jewish spouses and children, at least occasionally.

The vast majority of mixed-married households, however, are not unambiguously Jewish. Some form of Jewish holiday celebration is reported by over half of mixed-married families with one Jewish spouse. In mixed-married households that do not aim to be unambiguously Jewish, including the majority of families defining themselves as raising Jewish children, Jewish and Christian holiday activities are juxtaposed and interspersed.

The most ubiquitous Jewish activity is the Passover seder, which is attended, at least some of the time, by most American Jews regardless of marital status. Attendance at some type of Passover seder was a norm among mixed-married families with children. Many also had Hanukkah candles, festive dinners, or presents. Synagogue attendance, however, was not the norm. To compare two groups who both have Christian relatives, mixed-married families are only half as likely as conversionary or inmarried families to attend synagogue as part of their Jewish holiday activities, or to mark Jewish holidays beyond special meals for Passover, Hanukkah, and the fall High Holy Days.

Factors Associated with Increased Jewish Connections

Five characteristics are associated with extensive Jewish connections in mixed-married families: (1) Jews who received substantial formal Jewish education and/or who had positive, memorable Jewish experiences on a regular basis will often seek to replicate positive Jewish experiences in their own homes, especially after their children are born. (2) Families who meet and develop a relationship with a warm, supportive rabbi, Jewish educator, or other inspirational figure often undertake a journey of increasing closeness to Jewish activities. (3) Households in which the Christian spouse insists on a more intensive religious environment, even if that is a Jewish environment, often upgrade their Jewish involvements as years go on, provided that the Jewish partner is willing to become more Jewishly involved. (4) Jewish grandparents and other family members often serve as enrichment resources for mixed-married families. (5) Most significantly, households with Jewish mothers are more connected to Jewishness and less connected to Christianity in every measurable aspect of Jewish life than households with Jewish fathers.

Early religious experiences, whether through home-based practices or more formal, school-based educational settings, can have a belated effect during a family's religious evolutionary process. Geraldine Morris remembers that her parents weren't particularly observant, "but the whole family went to my grandparents' home every Friday night. We had candles and kiddush wine and all the blessings. Sometimes I went to the synagogue with my grandfather first. I really loved those Friday nights." For years after Geraldine married her non-Jewish husband, Kerry, they had few Jewish activities in their household. However, when her son turned three years old, she introduced weekly Shabbat celebrations into her household:

> At first it was kind of awkward, because it meant nothing to Kerry, and I hadn't had a strong enough background. But now it's something we all look forward to. I mean, it is our family time every week. We light the candles and we say the blessings of the candles, the wine, and the challah [special Sabbath bread]. And then, we usually try to say something good that happened that week, something we want to share with each other.

Although Geraldine's family does not currently belong to a synagogue, her early and informal Jewish education in the home of her grandparents has a profound influence on her behavior in her mixed family, and through her on the religious character of her household. Interview data such as hers demonstrate that educational experiences can have an impact—often unexpected—on Jewish connections long after their completion.

Mixed-married households are also more likely to incorporate regular Jewish activities into their family routines when they have a connection to a

Jewish leader whom they respect and feel close to. Many couples reported meeting a rabbi, often in connection with their planning a baby naming, with whom they established an increasingly deep connection. Surprisingly, the discovery of a personal religious mentor seems to be unrelated to who officiated at the wedding ceremony, as couples who found a religious mentor had a rabbi officiant, or both a rabbi and a Christian clergyman, or a non-religious officiant such as a family friend or justice of the peace. Even those who had rabbi officiants had usually since moved away from the geographical area in which they were married. The familial religious mentor, then, tended to be a person they had found later through some other, post-marriage avenue. Often either the birth of children or children's readiness for religious schooling serves as the motivation for finding a religious mentor.

Judy Connolly described the help that had been given to them by the rabbi of a temple near their home, and the influence that he and the synagogue community continue to exert on her family's lives. As Judy remembers:

> We heard about Rabbi Cohen through friends. He came to our home and explained the Jewish traditions about naming babies to us. He answered all our questions and was so patient with us. We had a really beautiful *bris* and baby naming for my oldest son, and then the same thing in our home for my second son. He helped us plan a baby naming for my daughter when she came also. So I think it is partly because of his influence that we are raising our children as Jews. We didn't think about religion much before we were married.

Chris Connolly offers one insight into why their consideration of the family's religious orientation didn't take place until their son was born: "You see, we weren't planning on having kids. Fortunately, it was an accident. We liked them so much we decided to have several. We would talk hypothetically about religion before we married, because like I said we weren't planning to have kids. But we did the *bris* for both baptisms. So we have decided to raise our kids as Jews."

The rabbi-mentor figure in the community turns out to be a far more important factor in a mixed-married family's connections to Judaism than whether or not a rabbi officiated at their wedding. Why is the rabbi-mentor such a significant figure in the creation of increased Jewish connections? A sympathetic and supportive rabbi is in a position to serve as a "broker" connecting mixed-married families to both Jewish activities and Jewish social networks (to use the language of social network theory). Through the rabbi as conduit, the mixed-married family constructs connections to Jewish information, holidays, and customs, thus acquiring more confidence in their own Judaic knowledge as well as more friends and acquaintances in the synagogue or school community. As the mixed-married family becomes more involved with a temple or school-based social network, their attitudes and expectations shift to more closely match those of the social network. Their increasing connection to Jewishness is thus embedded in the friendship group, as brokered by the rabbi.

The rabbi-mentor figure is seldom an officiating rabbi, because most couples do not settle in the location in which they got married. Study after study shows that the role of officiating clergy—rabbi, minister, or justice of the peace—actually has no statistical connection to the Jewishness—or lack of it—within the Jewish-Christian household. This is because the officiating rabbi, unlike the rabbi-mentor, usually does not serve as a conduit to Jewish social networks but instead renders a one-time service for the couple as a solo performance. Thus, although families often think of the officiating rabbi's role as supremely important, it is actually the rabbi-mentor in the temple or school community who serves as a meaningful bridge to Jewish identification.[12]

The third type of family situation that predisposes a mixed-married family to be Jewishly active involves the Christian spouse insisting on a meaningful religious framework of some type, whether Christian or Jewish. This spouse often agrees to raise the children as Jews but makes it clear even in the dating stage that the Jewishness of the household must consist of more than "going to temple three times a year," as Catherine Marshall said. "Jerry wasn't so keen on taking the children to services every Friday night, but he knew that either the children took their Jewish education and the holidays seriously or they went to catechism. So they know they are headed to bar mitzvah and we have a Jewish home." Interestingly, this type of sincere Christian spouse often also suggests that children are better off with one religious framework, rather than two, which they might find confusing.

In general, when Christian male or female spouses agreed to the celebration of Jewish, or a combination of Jewish and Christian, holidays, they usually cooperated fully with family celebrations. However, as noted earlier, some maintained internal reservations and looked forward to sharing them with their teenage children. The intergenerational dynamic was also evident in the fact that in more than one case, Jewish fathers reported having Christian holidays only in the homes of grandparents and other extended family members, while their teenage children reported that these festivities were sometimes held in their own homes.

Increase in Christian Observances over Time

Above all, holiday observances emerged as a process rather than a static condition in mixed-married households. There were dramatic differences in attitudes toward Christian holiday observances early in the marriage and after the passage of years. Jewish spouses, especially Jewish mothers, often began by establishing household rules about delegating Christian holiday celebrations to non-Jewish relatives. However, informants in their forties, whose parents were sometimes loosing the ability to host a holiday gathering, reported that holiday celebrations previously situated away from home had become their responsibilities. Thus, boundaries delineating the informant household as "Jewish" and the inlaw household as "Christian" blurred, and "Jewish" families with school-age children found themselves taking on increasing responsibility for Christian celebrations. By this point the Jewish spouse had often softened his/her resistance to the introduction of Christian practices into the household. As Gail Neely described it, "I love my mother-in-law, and she just can't do it any more. So now it's my pleasure to make Easter dinner for her and her family. I even make them a ham, because it means a lot to them. Except one year Easter fell on Passover, so I had them over for Easter dinner but I didn't make the ham."

Jewish spouses who had "won" the discussion over whose religion would be the primary religion of the household often felt guilty. They had empathy for what their spouses had given up. Jewish spouses who had insisted before marriage that their children must be brought up as Jews often became more and more concerned as the years passed that they were not being "fair" and had "taken too much away" from their fellow-traveler spouses. This guilty anxiety often became a vehicle for introducing or re-introducing Christian symbols into the household.

Shifts over time also occur when Jewish spouses find themselves enjoying Christian symbols and activities that previously felt alien to them. As Lee Gruzen points out in her book subtitled "How Interfaith Parents Can Give

Their Children the Best of Both Their Heritages," some Jews "realize" that some celebrations do not "violate" their "own Jewish identity" but instead show "respect" for "both Jewish and Christian traditions equally."[13]

In my study, similarly, one Jewish husband said he feels grateful that his non-Jewish wife has been "very good about sharing" the enterprise of creating a primarily Jewish home. He says he is also happy that "she has helped me compromise in terms of sharing her religion," especially with regard to "certain holidays, like Christmas, being able to celebrate that as a holiday, not so much as a religious holiday, but a social holiday."

Similarly, the Jewish wife of a non-Jewish husband who has been so well accepted by his Jewish inlaws that he has taken over the Jewish father-in-law's lucrative business said she feels badly that she has "deprived" her husband of a Christmas tree at home: "I don't want to be rigid. Now I make Christmas and Easter dinner for my mother-in-law, and the whole family goes to help friends decorate their Christmas trees. This year I bought a poinsettia for Cary—and also I bought it because it matches the kitchen. I don't think buying a poinsettia makes me any less Jewish." In order to make sure that her husband's Christian faith tradition is honored, she and her "raised Jewish" children attend at least one candlelit service during the year: "We used to go to the Unitarian church for that, but now our temple has a collaborative candlelight service the night before Thanksgiving in the Old North Church. It is beautiful. Also, I think it is important for my daughter to relate to her father's religion. She knows she's Jewish. I want her to understand what Christianity and Christmas are too."

Some families, like the Goldbergs, raise some children as Jews and some as Christians. This is especially common in "blended" households, in which the older children are products of an earlier, entirely Christian family. In the Goldberg household the daughter is being raised as a Catholic and the son as a Jew. The Catholic mother and her daughter place ashes on their foreheads at the appropriate time. The whole family has a seder, and the whole family goes to Easter mass and participates in an Easter dinner with bunnies and an egg hunt. In a particularly poignant demonstration of the intermingling of faith traditions, Jason Goldberg, their son, attends a community Jewish day school.

Jewish and Christian spouses sometimes had differing interpretations of the emotional significance of Jewish and Christian holiday symbols. As we have seen, Jewish parents often had squeamish feelings about Christian holiday symbols. On the other hand, many Christian spouses in this study described the Christian holidays as (1) American, (2) fun, (3) basically secular, and (4) manifestly normative. In contrast, the Jewish holidays were frequently described by Christian spouses as confusing, troublesome, too somber, or too religious:

> We celebrate Easter, which is a completely non-religious holiday . . . it's Easter eggs and bunnies . . . it's completely areligious and it's just a fun type thing. Then we do a seder. It's a pretty formal seder. . . . But you know, you go through a whole book, and everybody is complaining the whole way about going through the whole book. . . .
>
> And we do something on Rosh Hashanah. I always get a little bit confused about those holidays and what we're supposed to do, because it's less obvious than at the seder. Although it's getting a little bit clearer. . . . Don't do really much of anything on the Day of Atonement. Can't think of the name right now. . . . I need to keep track of when Yom Kippur is. . . .
>
> And then Christmas and Thanksgiving. Christmas looks like pretty much the average American Christmas. So it's got a Christmas tree. It's got lots of presents.
>
> Juliet has put her foot down recently that we not have lights outside the house. So there's kind of an interesting dynamic there. My kids kind of want to put some nice lights on the outside. And Juliet is saying, well, let's don't go to that extent, kind of a public display or something.

According to Mary Helene Rosenbaum, a founder of the Dovetail movement that supports dual-faith families, when interviewed on NBC's *Today Show* on July 10, 2001, many Jews, including intermarried Jews, have a surprisingly intense negative reaction to Christmas trees and external Christmas decorations. Ms. Rosenbaum explained that both Christmas trees and Easter eggs are not actually Christian but instead vestigial pagan practices. Given their pagan origins, according to Ms. Rosenbaum, it is irrational for Jewish partners and Jewish grandparents to oppose these activities, which are "cultural" rather than "religious."

Despite such rational analysis, cultural symbols have enormous power to evoke strong, and often unexpected, feelings. Charged with a historical overlay of acquired meaning, not the least of which are cultural "memories" (most of them taught, rather than directly experienced) of persecutions associated with Christmas and Easter, it was virtually irrelevant to many of the Jewish spouses interviewed whether rituals and ceremonies derived from pagan or Jewish or early Christian sources.

Thus, while readers may well wonder why researchers explore "just cultural" rituals such as a Christmas tree and Easter eggs, interview participants found weighty emotional significance within ceremonial moments in the life of the individual and the family. Christmas trees and Easter eggs may well be seen as lacking in spirituality, but for many Americans, whose lives contain relatively small amounts of religious ritual clustered mostly around life-cycle events and holiday seasons, the yearly holidays of mid-winter and emerging spring are high points of their religious lives and thus significant markers of the family's ethnoreligious identification.

6

LIFE-CYCLE EVENTS—I HOPE GOD HAS A SENSE OF HUMOR

If yearly holidays pack an emotional punch, life-cycle events such as birth ceremonies and bar and bat mitzvah celebrations—with their concomitant commitment to children's Jewish education—have the potential for seismic impact. The negotiation of ceremonies and rituals can serve as a useful laboratory for spouses who are trying to explore together how to create their family's ethnoreligious style. Sometimes they become a battleground for spouses with very different ideas about how they want to raise their children.

For many mixed-married couples, religious issues do not become particularly intense until their first child is born. Such couples often assume that their romantic feelings for each other can conquer their religious differences—until they find out that they really care about the birth ceremonies prescribed by their respective religions. These rituals provide potent examples that emotional responses to customs are not necessarily tied to their historic origins: one derivation for Christian baptismal water is the ancient Judaic immersion in the "living waters" of the *mikvah* (ritual bath). Nevertheless, Jewish parents and grandparents are almost universally aghast at the notion of Jewish children being baptized. To be baptized means to them that the child has been accorded entry into a community of the Christian faith; the Judaic genesis of the living waters is not a salient factor in the symbolic—and very Christian—meaning of baptism. Similarly, even those Christians who acquiesce to medical circumcision for hygienic reasons may feel queasy about the traditional Jewish communal celebration of the event, with bagels and lox waiting in the anteroom.

While many mixed-married couples have discussed religious birth ceremonies for their children prior to their births, not all of them manage to straighten out the logistics of their religious and affiliational lives enough to determine how to handle these early life-cycle events. Thus, one couple talked about the fact that they had not committed to a religious path at the time when birth ceremonies would have been appropriate:

> When Carl was born we really hadn't made any decisions about how we were going to raise our family, our kids. And by the time Jaqlyn was born two years later, we were a little more committed to raising the kids Jewish, but we hadn't really arrived there. So, it's something that friends of ours who are a mixed couple actually did have a *bris* for their son. But at that point, we really didn't realize we could do that.

Even spouses that love each other and inlaw families that get along well sometimes treat the negotiation of life-cycle events as a series of skirmishes in an ongoing battle for the ethnoreligious identity of the family. These skirmishes are often characterized by miscommunication between the spouses, accompanied by a striking difference of opinion over what particular events might mean.

Conversations with Gary and Crystalle Moskat about their son's ritual circumcision, for example, reveal two different narratives: Gary remembers that he wanted to maintain some sense of Jewish ritual without getting his young wife too upset. As he tells the story, his own ambivalence becomes clear, and he connects his ambivalence to his lack of Judaic knowledge: why fight for a traditional circumcision when he describes himself as not knowing its meaning or significance? From Crystalle's point of view, Gary's retreat on the issue of ritual circumcision gave her confidence that religious tradition really didn't matter much to Gary, and that he and his family would retreat on other religious issues as well.

The story begins with Gary's description of how he created what he calls a "mock *bris*":

> We talked about it and like having a *bris* with a *mohel,* having everybody here for eight days and all that stuff. And no one lives within a thousand miles of us. No relative lives within a thousand miles of us.
> And also I don't know what it means. You know, I don't know what a *bris*

means to me. I mean I know what it means, but I don't know what it means to me or to my life or anything like that. And I started reading *The Jewish Book of Why*. And was looking at circumcision and all those things and thought, you know, I hope God has a sense of humor, okay? Because here's what I think that I'm going to do. We'll have him circumcised. And I found some stuff about naming the child in a prayer book. I'll go in there and name the child after my dad and from what I've gathered from reading, you know, in the old days, the father was supposed to do the circumcision, but since they couldn't because they didn't have the skills to do it, they had a *mohel* to be a surrogate father. And you basically took in the surrogacy of performing the circumcision. So that's what I did to Rabbi Gonzales.

Doctor Gonzales was the doctor who I don't think was Jewish, but I told him he was for about fifteen minutes. And that he was my surrogate and that I would read a prayer while he did it. And he said I'm not the first one who's done it like this, which made me feel a little better. And we did the circumcision and, or he did the circumcision, and I read a prayer naming him and that was it. And I don't know if we'll do anything else. I don't know if we'll go to a Temple and have him named or anything like that. I'm not sure. But like I said, I hope God has a sense of humor.

The *brit milah* Gary didn't demand became an important sign of things to come for his wife, Crystalle. The unasked question is a very significant recurring motif in American Jewish life. For years, researchers looking at the lack of Jewish communal activism have heard interviewees say that they did not participate in particular activities because no one had asked them to do so. This dynamic is pronounced in mixed-married Jewish family life as well. From the largest issues to the smallest, many Jewish moments do not occur because the Jewish spouse or family member—often afraid of being too "pushy" or not "sensitive" enough—doesn't ask. Jewish spouses, and their parents, are often extremely uncomfortable with the implication that they are "forcing" their religion on an unwilling person.

Crystalle Quincy Moskat, who grew up in a lapsed Catholic home, said she was sure that her husband, Gary, would insist on a ritual circumcision. Although Gary was the fourth of four siblings in his family to marry a non-Jew, and she found his family very accepting of her, Crystalle had assumed that his family would attach a lot of importance to a traditional circumcision ceremony. She was surprised when her husband and his family did not insist on a *brit milah*.

As Crystalle put two and two together:

And so it doesn't seem like it's that important to him. I mean I thought when we had our son, I was thinking, oh, okay, the *bris,* that's going to be a big deal. For various reasons, I was not that interested in doing it. I mean partly just this like eight days after I'm home and having people in my house and the whole thing just seemed really—as it turned out, it was fine, I would have been fine after eight days with him. I couldn't imagine having people in my house and trying to organize any kind of an event or anything. And I just didn't feel comfortable with the whole thing and I thought, oh, he's really going to want it.

And when I brought it up and said, you know, I'm not that interested in doing that. I'd rather him circumcised in the hospital. He seemed okay with it. I thought for sure he'd say—if he had said, "No, it's really important to me that we do this and my mom cares," and whatever, I would have done it. I mean certainly there was no question that he would be circumcised. I mean I knew that was important to my husband. And so I didn't even look into the controversy over the whole thing because I just knew we were going to do that and that was fine. But he said, well, let's talk to my mom and see what she says.

And again, I was sure she was going to say we have to do it. She was going to be all disappointed. And she was basically, "Well, whatever you want to do, do whatever you want to do. And you can do a naming thing later if you want to do that. That's fine." She's pretty easygoing with that sort of a thing.

So because the family has that sort of attitude, I didn't feel like we needed to have extended conversations.

Connecting the conclusion of the *brit milah* episode with their current negotiations about the children attending Hebrew school, Crystalle concluded that Gary and his mother will not push for Hebrew school and a bar mitzvah, just as they did not push for a ritual circumcision:

I mean we've talked about things like is it important to you that the kids go to Hebrew school? More I guess the logistics. And because all of Gary's nieces and nephews so far have had bar or bat mitzvahs, so of course we've talked about affiliation with a school or temple to do that. And again, it's something that I'm not opposed to it, if he really wanted it, but I guess my choice would be that they would not do that. And Gary, at least at this point, seems to be fine with that. Maybe he'll change his mind when they come of age to do that sort of thing. But my vision is that neither of my kids will have a bat or bar mitzvah. If it becomes something that becomes important to him, I could be okay with it.

Crystalle Moskat said she bases her decision that her son and daughter will not attend Hebrew school partially on what she sees as her husband's failed religious education. She doesn't like the idea of their going to an after-school program twice a week to learn a foreign language, and she feels Hebrew school programs are ineffectual. When she thinks of her husband, Gary, she says, that it is clear that his years of Hebrew school "just taught him to read phonetically" and that "he doesn't know what the hell it means."

Certainly the afternoon Hebrew school feels alien to Crystalle's own childhood experiences. Although her family drifted from lapsed Catholicism into Unitarianism, the religious pattern she relates to is churchlike. She is most comfortable thinking about her children experiencing some form of Jewish education that feels more like a church: "I don't envision ever taking them to something, like, every Tuesday and Thursday during the week. So it wouldn't be Hebrew school per se, but I mean I'm assuming it would be like church where they have Sunday school for the kids while the parents are in the service."

Gary Moskat, meanwhile, is under the impression that he and Crystalle have decided that their children will receive a religious education that is similar to his own Hebrew school days. However, he readily admits that the religious environment that his children experience is very different from his own childhood experiences in New York, and later in his parents' Catskill Mountains resort. In the home he and Crystalle have created, Gary reflects, Jewish and Christian culture are "all mixed up together":

> I would say that they're getting Jewish culture and Christian culture. They're not hearing about Jesus Christ or things like that. I mean it's more of the Christmas and the Easter egg hunt and Christmas gifts and a Christmas tree and Santa Claus, which I know as a Jew it's a little hard to think my daughter is growing up believing in Santa Claus, but she is. And we haven't done Bible stories or anything like that with her yet. I imagine we will but they won't be with Jesus Christ being there. I guess Crystalle is Unitarian, if anything. And I don't think she's opposed to the Jewish schooling or something like that. We talked about Hebrew school. But we're not talking about going to church or anything like that.

In light of these recollections by Gary and Crystalle, it is not surprising that she was astonished at the continuing resistance of Gary and his family to home-based Christmas celebrations. The upcoming Moskat family negotiation over whether or not their children will receive formal Jewish education will no doubt comprise a formidable factor in whether or not their children will feel closely connected to their Jewish heritage in the years to come.

In American Jewish societies, Jewish education goes together with bar and bat mitzvah preparation like a "horse and carriage," to paraphrase an old song. Bar and bat mitzvah ceremonies in American communities today have a symbolic resonance that is different than in historic Jewish communities. While the bar mitzvah in traditional communities was often a comparatively low-key affair officially marking the passage of an adolescent boy into full adult religious responsibility, contemporary American bar and bat mitzvah ceremonies convey the impression that the celebrant is now joining the "club" of Jewish identification. Conversely, when an individual has not had a bar or bat mitzvah, he or she often feels somewhat less bona fide as a Jew. This feeling has been significant in the proliferation of adult bat mitzvahs in communities across the United States.[14]

This contemporary symbolic valence helps to explain the popularity of bar and bat mitzvah events among our mixed-married informants, at least in their planning stages. More than one-fifth of mixed-married informants had already given their son and/or daughter a bar or bat mitzvah ceremony, and the great majority said they were planning such an event. Although the majority of mixed-married couples reported that they were aiming to give their children bar or bat mitzvah ceremonies, many of them were also critical about such events.

It was common for both Jews and non-Jews to speak harshly about materialism in the Jewish community, and these critiques were often focused on Jewish institutional or life-cycle events. One Jewish man commented that, if it were up to him, his sons would not have bar mitzvahs, but his Christian wife insists that their "Jewish" upbringing must include some religious content:

> Recently, my older brother's son was bar mitzvahed and, you know, I just see so much hypocrisy in religion in general that I would feel like kind of a hypocrite. My bar mitzvah wasn't a particularly enriching experience, and I'm not sure that any thirteen-year-old boy's ever has been other than they got lots of really cool Cross pens. . . . Cecilia's position is that unless I can become more involved in Judaism, then it's not fair for me to expect our kids to be, and I'm not sure that I'm willing to make that commitment.

Nevertheless, it is important to recognize that, for many American Jewish parents, giving one's children a Jewish education and a bar or bat mitzvah is one of the most significant ways of expressing one's own Jewish commitments. This is true of mixed-married households that give their children a Jewish education, just as it is true of inmarried and conversionary households. Indeed, the symbolism of a bar or bat mitzvah in a mixed-married family is often profound, given the cultural "meaning" of these occasions in America. The bar/bat mitzvah event becomes a graphic demonstration to the extended Jewish family and community that the Jewish partner has indeed "produced" a Jewish child and has thus been faithful to the historical concept of creating a Jewish household.

In households that are deliberately raising children with an interfaith or dual-faith religious tradition, the meaning of bar/bat mitzvah sometimes becomes transformed into a declaration of Judaic commitment. Participants in the Dovetail Institute for Interfaith Family Resources Conference (Chicago, 2002) spoke about the interfaith schools that their children attended. These schools, their religious attitudes and activities, and the social networks that they provide comprise a defined society with which Dovetail families identify. The double religious commitments of Dovetail families are embedded in their interfaith school societies and friendship circles.

When these children reach the age of thirteen, they have a "coming of age" ceremony that blends religious traditions, presided over by the rabbi and the priest associated with their school. Only those children who have decided that they want to be unequivocally Jewish have a ceremony called a bar/bat mitzvah in these interfaith schools. Becoming a bar/bat mitzvah means renouncing the Christian piece of the family heritage and "becoming" a Jew, in this milieu.

One young teenager, Kevin Novick, spoke about the reasons he had decided not to have a bar mitzvah. Throughout his childhood he had attended both church schools and interfaith Jewish temple schools. He had received first and second communion in the Catholic church. His family attended services both in temples and in the Catholic church during the yearly holiday cycle. "I was really thinking about having a bar mitzvah," said Kevin,

A lot of my friends had bar mitzvahs, and I really wanted it because it's such a cool day. You're the center of attention, there's a great party, and you get all those presents. But then I spoke to the rabbi at my [interfaith] school, and he explained to me that being bar mitzvah meant taking on the obligation to do all those Jewish things every week. And I'm really not ready to say that I'll do Shabbat every week, and that I'll go to temple and pray. So I'm not ready to say I'm only going to have one religion. So I decided not to have a bar mitzvah.

"Maybe," he added wistfully, "when I grow up and meet someone I love and want to marry her, then I'll decide to have only one religion. Because what if the woman I love is a Buddhist or a Hindu or something? I don't think it would work to raise kids in three religions, so I'll have to choose one, and then we'll have two religions in our family."

Kevin's conviction of the feasibility of having two—but not three—religions in a household goes back to his own birth. Josh Nozick described how he and his wife, Katie, talked about and went back and forth on how to raise the children before his son was born. Then, while Katie was in labor with their first child, he ran into a "right wing" rabbi whose wife was in the next labor room. After Josh described to this rabbi how he and Katie were struggling with the raising of their children, the rabbi told him, "Go ahead and raise your children as Catholics, Josh. The Jewish people can do without you and your children."

So Josh went into the labor room and told Katie, who was pushing and panting, "Katie, I think we should raise him as a Catholic." Katie gasped out, "I don't think this is a good time to discuss this, dear." The Nozicks decided to raise their children in two religions, Catholicism and Judaism, and were among the founding members of their Catholic-Jewish dialogue group. They think of themselves as a principled dual-faith family. For their children, two religions are the family tradition. Over the years, Katie's greater knowledge about and affection for her own Catholicism, compared to Kevin's ignorance and ambivalence about Jews and Judaism, has conveyed itself to their children. As in the case of Gary and Crystalle Moskat, the lack of passion Jewish spouses show for Judaism has an important impact on the ethnoreligious family dynamic. All the "not askings" add up and teach non-Jewish spouses that Jewish things are "not that important."

7

YOURS, MINE, AND OURS

Husbands and wives in mixed-married families often feel that they are involved in an ongoing process of negotiating and juggling "yours, mine, and ours" religious identities. Gender often becomes an important determining factor in these negotiations. The presence—or absence—of a Jewish mother is a strong predictor of the extent of Jewish identification and behavior in a given household. National data repeatedly show that mixed-married homes with Jewish mothers score higher on every measure of Jewish connectedness, including social and affiliational measures as well as Jewish education for the children and ritual observance. Our interview data provide real stories that explain why the presence of a Jewish woman in the household is so significant. A Christian woman's voice opposing the circumcision of her newborn baby, for example, is difficult for many Jewish husbands to oppose. Moreover, woman are often the delegated carpool drivers, and a mother who does not wish to have her children attend afterschool Judaic supplementary classes (Hebrew school or Talmud Torah) can quite effectively scuttle plans for a Jewish education. Women in many households are still also often the designated cooks and may not wish to fuss with special meals for Sabbaths or Jewish holidays. Not least, women are often the social planners for the family and can construct the family's social life around other Jewishly connected families—or not. Jewish women are most often the conduit to the family's Jewish social networks.

Carmen Moslowky, a Brazilian woman who describes her own ethnic heritage as "Arabic, Portuguese, Spanish, and French," hated her Catholic up-bringing in a strict community. She is nevertheless determined that her children will be raised with a blend of both her husband's Judaism and her Catholicism. Her husband is not comfortable with the level of Christianity she has incorporated into the family, says Carmen, but she wants to provide her children with the flavor of their material ethnoreligious heritage. As Carmen explained her viewpoint, she emphasized the external fungibility of ethnic backgrounds:

> People who know me superficially believe I'm Jewish. I can pass as Jewish for a long time before they find out. My next door neighbor is the wife of a rabbi. She found out only two months ago. Something happened in her house that was really extreme, and I said, "Oh, my God!" She said, "You're not Jewish, are you?" And then she came over to my house, and there were Christmas decorations and stuff, the St. Francis of Assisi there! . . .
>
> The idea was, like, we'd expose them to both, and then when they'd grow up they can decide. And fortunately I'm easy with that because I had parents with different views of religion. And when I grew up I made my own decision. Jake is not so comfortable with the Catholicism part of the bringing up. But what I want to pass to my children is very simple, actually. God is just one. And religions are just different ways to love the same God. And you do your best in life, and that's all. And you don't do to other people what you don't want them to do to you. . . .
>
> We do candles, and dreidel games, and stories of Hanukkah for Meredith. Passover we had a special dinner, a kosher one, no less. On Christmas we have a tree, and we have all the ornaments, and we have the Christmas Eve special dinner. And we put out cookies for Santa Claus. And on Easter, we have eggs—and that's when Meredith gets converted! Anything with chocolate, Meredith converts to Christianity immediately!

In homes where ethnoreligious identity has been left unresolved, Christian mothers often lobby for the incorporation of Christian observances into the household, or at least for lesser levels of Jewish education for the children, and they have an impact even in cases where Jewish husbands have positive feelings about Jewish education and identity. Christian resistance to "too much" Jewish schooling is even more effective, of course, when Jewish husbands have ambivalent feelings about Jewish education. Indeed, Christian spouses are not infrequently cited as the "cover" for what is clearly the Jewish spouse's issues with Jewish identity.

Josh Mendlowitz said about his wife, "Whatever Christina wants, Christina gets," for example, and then made it clear that he shares many of Christina's reservations about Jewish education:

> I'd like to think that we work things out as a couple. I respect Christina an enormous amount, and I think our values are pretty together. We want the same things, and we want the same things for our kids.
>
> But I felt that I was going to sacrifice my generation and I was willing to do that if my children would be brought up as Jews. Passing on the legacy is very important to me. It means a lot to me that we were the inheritors of this faith that has gone on for thousands of years, and I feel that we've brought so much to the world. And I felt like at least if I'm going to betray something, at least if our kids are Jewish, there's a fighting chance that the next generation could be saved. . . .
>
> I never asked that Christina convert. I don't feel it's appropriate to do that, particularly someone in Christina's situation who grew up in a Catholic family. . . .
>
> We worry about the kids getting too much Jewish school. What the heck is the best way to say this—if they need that kind of steady immersion, I mean if every single day they get half an hour of Torah and an hour of Hebrew and so forth, it gets to the point where they're not even bar mitzvahed and they're burned out. I mean I guess I'd rather see them a little more moderate in everything. We have them in school Saturday and Sunday mornings, but soon we are going to stop on the Saturdays.

Although Josh believes himself committed to "passing on the legacy" and giving his children a strong attachment to Jewishness, he is deeply convinced that Jewish education is intrinsically unattractive. His notion of "immersion" in Jewish education amounts to under two hours a day, and he imagines that children who are subjected to this level of Judaica on a regular basis will quickly be "burned out." In comparison, it is very unlikely for parents to say that children who read English "an hour a day" will be "burned out" by the time they reach age thirteen.

The ambivalence of the Jewish father is at least as salient a factor as the convictions of the Christian mother in undermining the Jewish character of some mixed-married households, as Josh's words reveal. The impact of a non-Jewish mother may be especially pronounced also because non-Jewish mothers are more likely to stay home with young children than Jewish mothers.

Contrary to some popular misconceptions, husbands and wives in inmarried Jewish families tend to occupy higher educational and occupational statuses, as a group, than in mixed-married households, according to 1990 NJPS data. Moreover, Moshe and Harriet Hartman found that strong levels of Jewish connectedness are "not associated with more spousal inequality." The Hartmans conclude:

> The elements in the Jewish religion that emphasize the reciprocal and equivalent nature of the husband and wife duties and obligations, which support an active economic role for wives, and the long tradition of secular achievement of both Jewish men and women counteract any spillover that might have been expected from the unequal ritual roles accorded to men and women in the Jewish religion.[15]

College students who come from mixed-married families are far more likely to identify themselves as Jews if they have a Jewish mother rather than a Jewish father. A new study of America's Jewish freshmen provides stunning statistics. Mixed-married freshmen with Jewish mothers were more than twice as likely to identify as Jews as those with Jewish fathers. Of those freshmen having a Jewish mother and a non-Jewish father, 38 percent identified as Jews. Of those having a Jewish father and a non-Jewish mother, only 15 percent identified as Jews. Mixed-married freshmen with Catholic mothers were the least likely to identify as Jews—12 percent. Those with Jewish mothers and non-identifying non-Jewish fathers were the most likely to identify as Jews—47 percent.[16]

Non-Jewish spouses also spoke of aspects of Jewishness that they disliked or resented. Although they cooperated with the Jewish logistics of their children's lives, many grew to resent being "shut out" of these important rituals. Few of them wanted to learn Hebrew—some had tried!—but they disliked the fact that their children were learning a language they did not know. Since they no doubt would not have had the same resentful feelings about their children learning French, Spanish, or Italian, it is clear that in these cases Hebrew has attained a symbolic salience and may represent the whole package of religious dislocation that these spouses feel but do not often articulate.

On an ideological level, many non-Jewish spouses said they resented what they perceived as the exclusivity of Judaism as a religion. Significantly, very few Christian spouses said they had been treated coldly in synagogues, Jewish institutions, or Jewish social settings. Their notion of the exclusivity of Judaism was related to ideas about Jews as "the chosen people." Thus, they talked about their impressions that Jews as a group "want to be separate" or "want to be different." However, when pressed, even those who had been coldly treated by Jewish families insisted that Jewish institutions had not offended them.

The relative lack of stories about being turned away by Jewish institutions was, no doubt, influenced by the fact that Jewish spouses often served as troubleshooters, investigating the policies of temples and schools before bringing their Christian spouses into them or enrolling their children. In other words, Jewish institutions with policies that exclude mixed-married families and their children certainly exist, but many mixed-married families avoid them by doing research and only connecting up with institutions with more inclusionary policies.

Many Christian spouses were offended by aspects of Judaism as a system of values and behaviors. Several non-Jewish spouses, especially Christian men, expressed resentment about Jewish religious rituals being too behavioristic and external instead of being simply matters of belief. Some explicitly spoke disparagingly about "legalism" or "too much attention to details instead of larger, more important ethical issues."

One Christian husband heatedly criticized an acquaintance who avoided eating pork. "Why do Jews have to invent laws about not eating pork?" he demanded. "Why don't they pay attention instead to the express, literal word of God in the Bible?" When asked what he thought that was, he simply repeated, "They should pay attention to the express, literal word of God in the Bible." Another Christian husband focused his irritation with Jewish legalism on the fact that many Jewish men wear head coverings (*kippah* or *yarmulkeh*) in the synagogue or at home-based religious occasions:

> The respect I have is in my heart. It shouldn't be symbolized by what I have on my head. It's true from the heart and nothing that needs an outward sign. I'm in defiance against the idea that if I already have something in my heart I have to wear a *yarmulkeh* to prove it. I don't think that because Jewish men will wear that as a sign of respect to God that I have any less respect for God by not wearing it. Especially when you think about other religions that don't wear *yarmulkehs*—Christians—who sit there not wearing *yarmulkehs*, but they have no less respect for God.

Another man said he could never become a Jew because "Jewish culture has never produced an original thinker. Any Jewish philosophy is derivative."

A dislike of organized religion in general was pronounced among some non-Jewish spouses. They said that religion was important in raising children because it gives them structure and a moral framework, but that adults were probably better off without religion. They said they were waiting until their children "are old enough to understand what's wrong with organized religion," and then they were going to share their reservations with their children. For many of them, this desire to tell adolescent children that they don't really need religion was related to stories of their own "emancipation" from their religious faith at some point during adolescence.

Just as the process of juggling two faith traditions often begins very early in the history of the family or in the pre-family period, for many mixed-married families it is a neverending story. One common motif in ongoing familial religious negotiations is the "change of heart." One or the other spouse agrees that the child should be raised in a particular way but at some point in the marriage undergoes a kind of transformative experience, making the original decision untenable to him or her.

Connie Mosher, a raised-Catholic woman married to a Jewish man, for example, had not thought that raising the children as Christians was very important to her before her children were born and when they were small. This was partially because she found herself "turned off" by Catholic classes, which she characterized as "really a lot of just games." However, about ten years ago she and a female friend were "exposed to a small Bible church at the corner of my street" that she found far more appealing. As a result, "my one girlfriend and I are now born-again Christians." Connie has been sending her children to the church's "vacation Bible school" for "this kind of, you know, Bible-based religious instruction."

Sometimes, in contrast, the Christian spouse becomes more interested in Judaism as time goes on. This does not always make the Jewish spouse happy. Jack Magencey explained that at first he felt quite liberal about his wife's Christianity: "Candy and I have been to church twice in eight years. Do I prevent, deny, say to her she shouldn't? Absolutely not. I encourage her to do what I consider in her heart. I say, whatever is in your heart is the right thing, and you should do it. If you want to go to church, go. I'll be happy to watch my sports things on Sunday." When Candy became attracted to Jewish religious communal activities, however, Jack reacted far less comfortably and dropped his laissez faire posture: "Candy goes to Passover seder. Candy is more Jewish than I am, a factor that has annoyed me. I said to her, why are you getting involved with all these Jewish organizations? It's annoying. I married a Christian who is now running around with the Jews—and I avoid them like the plague!"

Even when both spouses have agreed to raise the children in one religion, the spouse whose religion was not chosen often dreams about giving children more information about his or her religious background. Interview participants spoke not only about discussions in the past and in the present, but even about those they anticipated having in the future. Kenneth Morris, the father of three Jewish school-age children, thought he would tell them about his Christian roots when they became teenagers:

> I would explain to them my history, my parents and all that, when they get older. I imagine that when they get into their early teen years, then that's when I'd probably have to. Because I know it's going to come up.
>
> "And why isn't Dad Jewish? Why aren't you Jewish?"
>
> I don't think of myself as a Christian. I believe in a higher power and that's pretty much it. And so to sit down and explain to them what I think and what I believe, why. Yes. When the time is right, that will come up. And I want them to. I want them to know and, I guess, have respect for it. . . . From early on I want them to understand that there are other religions out there, and to me religion is not an issue of right or wrong, it's rather an issue of inner peace.
>
> I want them to understand that. I want them to grow up, you know, not being prejudiced against Indians or Buddhists or whatever.

Of course, ongoing religious negotiations are not exclusive to mixed-married families. Inmarried families also frequently negotiate and renegotiate religious postures within the family. Conversionary households also are often involved in an ongoing discussion about their religious behavior. Some of this discussion arises around issues of how ritually observant the family will be. An inmarried Conservative family that decides to send their children to Jewish day school, or to become more firmly committed to the observance of the kosher dietary laws, often encounters anger or rebellion on the part of grandparents or one or more of the children. Some of these encounters can be quite charged with emotions, even though both families ostensibly descend from the same faith traditions.

For mixed-married couples, however, the chasm between the religious

backgrounds of their two families can often seem more potentially danger-
ous or intimidating in terms of the potential to disrupt established lifestyles.
Janet Morris, a Jewish mother, is pleased that "we keep a Jewish house" that
does not include a Christmas tree—a decision made "before we got married." However, she worries that Kenneth, her second gentile husband, may
someday renege on their agreement, as her first husband, Christopher, did:

> One of my biggest fears was when a baby comes, that Kenneth would turn
> out just like Christopher, and be, like, all of a sudden scared. You know, I would
> be like three years down the road and he would say, "You're going to hell." And
> Kenneth was, like, you know, "No, that's not going to happen." He used to re-
> assure me and reassure me, and I don't believe he will. There's no guarantee—
> I just don't know, you know. After many years.

Janet would feel more comfortable if Kenneth would agree to convert,
but she doesn't think he ever will:

> But I also don't think that he will adopt any sort of religion, like it would be
> nice if he were Jewish. Okay, I know it would be nice for me too. But mainly
> for the kids. Because he really does his philosophy, as in Jewish philosophy.
> And spirituality. I would have to say that I don't know if Kenneth wouldn't con-
> vert just because of the stuff to convert, or if it's really like a basic thing that I-
> just-can't-do-it sort of thing.

The holidays that mark the calendar year, returning annually with com-
forting familiarity, and the moments that transform personal life, such as
birth, marriage, and death, and the ceremonies that mark personal rites of
passage, such as bar and bat mitzvah, loom large in personal maps of meaning. Indeed, recurring holidays and the sacralization of life-cycle events are
probably the most significant aspects of religion to most Americans, regardless of religious or marital status.

Our interview data indicate that many American Jews experience communal life-cycle ceremonies as manifestations that their personal transitions
are important to friends, family, and community. They say that, in a religious
setting, such ceremonial events make them feel that their personal transitions are connected to historical Jewish communities and to some concept of
divinity, whatever they perceive the relationship to be between themselves,
the Jewish people, and God. It is thus not surprising that Jewish families, in-

cluding many mixed-married couples, strive to find modes to bring the various social networks of their families and community together to mark their important life passages in some ceremonial way.

Inmarried and conversionary Jewish couples usually build upon venerable Jewish formulas, and mixed-married couples are also often interested in adapting these ceremonies for the particular needs of their family groups. In one of the most ancient of Jewish traditions, infants are initiated into the covenant of the Jewish people through the *brit milah* for boys; today, many infant girls are named and/or welcomed at newly popular shalom bat ceremonies. These events are extremely meaningful to parents, siblings, and extended families. Since most growing children become fascinated by pictures and stories of themselves, one may even say that these initiation events eventually have meaning for the children themselves.

As children enter puberty, American bar and bat mitzvah ceremonies have pride of place in Jewish family life, absorbing the entire family in elaborate planning and compelling young adolescents to engage in months of preparations. In addition, stable rates of Jewish education for boys and rising rates of Jewish education for girls are closely tied into the ubiquitousness of bar and bat mitzvah in American Jewish communities. Mixed-married families also draw on these historical Jewish models, but many of them simultaneously negotiate, revise, and merge two or more ethnoreligious traditions. In this process of syncretic inventing of new traditions, many mixed-married families are aided by the popular, paradoxical American trend of celebrating ethnoreligious differences as testimony to the sameness of all Americans. Americans share the experience of deriving from diverse, particularistic heritages, and the contemporary liberal ethos simultaneously accentuates and transcends differences. Valorizing the differences that unite, liberal Americans are fond of emphasizing commonalities that seem to span ethnic and religious boundaries.

Teens with Two Traditions

Children that grow up in mixed-married households do not share their parents' memories. They are shaped by the new memories their parents have provided for them. The holiday sequences they participate in, and the life-cycle events they experience, come to shape the world of their expectations.

When parents feel ambivalent about their religious commitments, teenagers are quick to pick up on that sense of ambivalence. Thus teenagers growing up in mixed-married homes who participated in this study's focus groups sometimes described the religious character of their households in ways that were at odds with their parents' descriptions. "My folks like to deny the fact that we do Christmas as home," said one sixteen-year-old. "Each time it happens they say there's a particular reason. But it happens more years than they like to admit."

Some teenagers are raised in principled interfaith households—that is, households that conscientiously blend two or more religious traditions. At the Dovetail Conference held in Chicago in 2002, several teenage children of interfaith households spoke about the ways they had been raised, and how they now interpreted and felt about their religious beliefs. The Dovetail teenagers had often absorbed the clearly delineated interfaith value systems in which they were inculcated. They had a lively appreciation of comparative religious beliefs and seemed to exhibit a high tolerance for ambiguity. Indeed, many of them felt that the tolerance for ambiguity they had been taught gave them important life skills.

Several of the children suggested that, in their experience, "children can accept many complicated things as normal." They emphasized that children do not necessarily share expectations that are common in the outside world. For example, Cerise Manischwitz said that when she was very young she asked her mother, "Is Jesus God?" Her mother thought for a moment and then answered, "I believe Jesus is God, and Daddy doesn't." Cerise responded by asking again, "Yes, but is Jesus God?" This time her mother responded, "I believe Jesus is God, and Daddy doesn't, and when you grow up you can decide for yourself." Cerise continued: "And that just made perfect sense to me. It just fit, and it seemed totally normal, and I was okay with it."

Most of the children said they considered themselves "interfaith" or "having two faiths." They said that they "weren't confused," and that they were "lucky" to have two religions. Cerise said she thought children raised with only one religion are more at risk for disillusionment and dropping religion all together. Cerise felt that being raised to understand that all religious knowledge is relative protects one against being disillusioned by the discovery that one's religion is not unique, or is flawed, or is threatened by scientific thinking. She continued, "If you have only one religion and you believe in it very strongly, then if you stop believing in it you have nowhere to go. But we always have another religion to turn to. And besides, we are raised to look at religions in comparison with each other. So we know that if one 'truth' turns out not to feel like the truth to us, there are other versions of the truth we can think about and maybe believe in."

Fascinatingly, out of the four teenagers on a panel who had been identically brought up in an interfaith Catholic-Jewish worship and dialogue community, only one had chosen to identify as a Jew: Sara, whose Catholic mother works for the church. Cerise, her older sister, has had each of her communions but not a bat mitzvah. Cerise said she views her religious life as a journey. Now she spends more time in the church than the synagogue. On the other hand, she attends a Torah study class on her Ann Arbor college campus each week. She said she "loves" the readings, which are eclectic, and the discussion.

In contrast, her younger sister, Sara, said she never felt comfortable in the church. She told her parents as a schoolgirl that she didn't want to go to church anymore, and that she wanted to attend Hebrew school. Her father responded, "Why do you want to do that, Sara? I hated Hebrew school!" Nevertheless, she insisted, and they enrolled her. Sara still attends temple but not church, and she thinks of herself as Jewish. She said she once spoke to a person who helps individuals access their "previous existences," and Sara is convinced that factors from a previous existence have influenced her to choose Jewishness. In yet another example of the ambivalence of a Jewish spouse, the Jewish father (who hardly said a word during the presentation and discussion) has been fully supportive of his daughters attending church school but tried to dissuade Sara from going to Hebrew school.

What is the sociological significance of the ethnoreligious and cultural syncretism that characterize American mixed marriages between Jews and non-Jews today? This question is profoundly complex, partially because conceptions of ethnicity underwent sweeping changes during the second half of the twentieth century. Constructionist theories of ethnicity encourage us to view ethnicity as fluid, as continually being negotiated and renegotiated.[17] If we accept the main tenet, that race and ethnicity are social constructs based on perceptions of difference created by persons both internal and external to the group, it seems clear that new notions of ethnoreligious identity are being pieced together in many mixed-married households. The blended cultures found in many such households differ from premodern, rabbinic Jewish communal norms. To a degree not always appreciated, contemporary mixed-married households also differ strikingly in their syncretism from attitudes and behaviors along the continuum of normative American Reform, Reconstructionist, Conservative, Traditional, and Orthodox Judaism.

American Jewish rejection of the overt blending of Jewish and Christian religious traditions is symbolized and reflected in our informants' insistence that "Jewish is different." The fact that inmarried and (to a slightly lesser extent) conversionary Jewish households avoid Christian holiday celebrations in their own homes is a powerful testimony to their willingness to be different. Despite a heavily advertised Christmas shopping season that now begins in early November, despite strong cultural messages that all religions are really the same, despite reported Jewish acceptance of actual or potential intermarriages among friends and family members, men and women in households with a single, Jewish religious identity still seem to agree with Robert Bellah's statement, "It is part of Jewish identity and the maintenance of the boundaries of the Jewish community to deny that Jesus is the Christ."[18]

Some social scientists emphasize the importance of boundaries in creating distinct ethnic groups.[19] Distinctiveness is maintained by these boundaries, they argue, although the content of the distinctiveness changes.[20] Betting on the effectiveness of boundaries, however, would seem a risky choice for those concerned with American Jewish distinctiveness today, because the vast majority of Americans enjoys the enormous benefits of tolerance promoted by increasingly porous and permeable social boundaries.

In contrast, rather than boundary maintenance, the "cultural stuff" at the heart of ethnic group life and "the nuclei, the centers of ethnic culture" are what nourishes dynamic group distinctiveness and cohesiveness, according to another sociological approach.[21] Richard Alba and others find that interest in ethnicity is actually greater and more persistent among highly educated and socioeconomically successful white ethnic Americans; the more educated and successful the white American, the more interested she or he is in passing an ethnic identity along to the next generation.[22] It seems likely that mixed-married couples, like other American Jewish families, will continue to be interested in some forms of Jewish activities in their homes, because they fit overwhelmingly into this demographic.

The voices of our interview participants suggest that the majority of mixed-married families has not only crossed previously significant ethnoreligious boundaries but is also involved in an ongoing revision of the nucleus-core Judaic attitudes, values, and behaviors. The great divide between all-Jewish inmarried and conversionary families and partly Jewish mixed-married households is reflected in the presence of Christian symbols and activities in the home. Avoiding Christian activities in their homes still seems to be the bottom line for most American Jews. Given demographic trends, this attitudinal and behavioral stance may be a transitional phenomenon. Researchers do not yet know what the impact will be on American Jewish societies and on communal and religious life when adults who have grown up in households not characterized by this visceral avoidance of Christian holiday and life-cycle observances become an ever more substantial percentage of the greater American Jewish community. However, an examination of Jewish secular and religious communal responses to mixed-married families (chapters 9 and 10) shows that they are already having an important effect on American Jewish life.

III

MIXED MARRIAGE IN
CULTURAL CONTEXTS

8

INTERFAITH ROMANCE IN LITERATURE, FILM, AND POPULAR CULTURE

Parts I and II of this book focused on the narratives told by the men and women my study interviewed about their intercultural courtships and marriages. Most people saw their experiences as highly personal and individualistic—unlike those of anyone else. However, personal decisions are often influenced both by the norms of a person's social networks and also by the values supported by the general cultural environment in which one lives.

Social norms and cultural expressions sometimes conflict with each other. New behaviors and ideas are frequently explored through cultural venues before they are widely espoused by mainstream social networks. Creative writers often depict innovative cultural concepts and show how social networks resist these new ideas. For example, the symbolism of intercultural marriages long outstripped their actual occurrence in American societies. Although exogamy faced resistance both from Christian societies and also from many minority groups, including Jews, stories about intercultural love have been a recurring—and apparently appealing American theme.

Contemporary behaviors have now caught up to artistic visions. To a sometimes startling extent, my study's real-life informants told stories that had striking parallels to the plots, motifs, and characters of literature, film, and popular culture. Creative writers often seem to be prescient, because they are free to describe social phenomena before they become statistically measurable. Without conducting a study and interviewing informants, novelists and screenwriters can delve into behaviors and their symbolic significance.

These creative works can provide important clues to the social scientist studying the tenor of the times and trying to gain an understanding of evolving trends.[1]

Thus, by paying attention to the popularity of 1920s plays and films like *The Jazz Singer* (1927) and *Abie's Irish Rose* (1929), we can see that long before intermarriage between Jews and non-Jews grew into a large, statistically important phenomenon, the idea of Jewish-Christian affection had positive symbolic significance both for Jews and the larger American population. In addition to these overt—and positive—presentations of Jewish Christian pairs, cross-racial and cross-cultural love was championed in novels such as Edna Ferber's *Showboat,* later a Jerome Kern and Oscar Hammerstein musical, released as a film in 1936, and Rogers and Hammerstein's *South Pacific,* a musical drama transforming James Michener's stories, which was released as a film in 1958. In each of these artistic creations, the ability of minority groups to marry persons from mainstream culture is presented as a test of whether democratic ideals reign in American lives. Created largely by Jews, each of these novels, plays, and films was in its own way an encoded story about a romantic liaison that enabled a Jew to pass across ethnoreligious lines.

One of the most powerful American cinematic images of interfaith romance is also one of the earliest. *The Jazz Singer* mesmerized audiences at a time when ethnic immigrants were expected to acculturate as completely and quickly as possible. It argues that in order to become a real American, the Jew must translate his personal and professional passions into the American idiom. Interfaith romance is presented as the venue for doing that.

In *The Jazz Singer*'s climax on Kol Nidrei evening, Al Jolsen, as Jack Robins, the cantor's son, appears in blackface, flanked by his dowdy, weeping mother on one side and his quintessentially Christian sweetheart—a beautiful dancer provocatively clad in spangles, feathers, and dangling earrings—on the other. He must choose between the diverging values and socioeconomic statuses they represent.

Jewish tradition, in the bearded, rotund person of Cantor Rabinowitz, is portrayed throughout the film as rigid, parochial, anachronistic, self-absorbed, and vindictive. Perhaps worst of all, ethnoreligious fidelity allows no freedom to the individual to determine his own path in life. "What has he to say about it?" Rabinowitz thunders about his son's musical profession. "For five generations Rabinowitzes have been cantors." Cantor and Mrs. Rabinowitz embody ghettoized tenement life—and the giving up of everything America has to offer.

On the other hand, May MacAvoy tells Jolson that the theater is "the place God has put you." This glittering non-Jewish woman represents the wide world of American opportunity, a meritocracy in which talent and energy can wipe out centuries of persecution. Choosing his non-Jewish girlfriend will allow Jolsen to pass into a new race and a new class. The non-Jewish woman gives the Jewish man a chance to become white, winning, and wealthy. Robins (and Jolsen) can hardly be blamed for being alienated by his father's forbidding, repressive, and backward set of religious customs, and for choosing a non-Jewish woman over the faith of his fathers.

As Jolson's character makes his choice, his blackface takes on a multilayered symbolism. Historically, Jews were important middlemen in bringing African American jazz music to the attention of a wider audience, often while wearing blackface.[2] On a deeper level, the dark greasepaint and nappy wig hint at the putative "racial" difference that was often assigned to the "Jew's body" in antisemitic writings, as Sander Gilman has chillingly demonstrated.[3] Jack Robins moans repeatedly that he hears the "cries of my race" calling to him, urging him to sing "the songs of my people." If he chooses his parents, he will in fact be rejoining an Old Country race, and the outsider's status that goes along with it. On the other hand, by appearing as a black American, Robins becomes "unrecognizable as a Jew," masked and thus exempted from the Hebrew race.[4] Paradoxically, "by identifying with blacks, Jews were at home in America" in a way that they could not be as overt Jews for many decades to come.[5]

The Jazz Singer sets the stage for the continuing valorization of interfaith romances. A non-Jewish love interest is repeatedly presented as the implement and symbol of American success for the American Jewish man. The Jewish woman, in contrast, is portrayed as less American and often a potentially formidable obstacle to a man's progress and personal happiness. By singing a Jewish song, the protagonist allies himself with a backward people and culture; by singing a jazz song with a non-Jewish woman, he joins the universalistic world of Western arts and culture. This familial plot and its accompanying themes may make some readers think of Joel Millstein, who expressed his independence from "stifling" Jewish expectations by first acquiring a German musical instrument, then studying music in Austria, and eventually marrying an upper-class Episcopalian woman.

Gendered Depictions and Their Implications

When viewers recognize characters in film or television as "Jewish," one reference point is a cultural, literary, and cinematic tradition, including popular fiction and Hollywood films, that promulgates Jewish stereotypes. These "Jewish" film images, in turn, often echo stereotypes of Jews that developed during earlier historical periods and settings. Antisemitism created grotesque caricatures that Diaspora Jews internalized from Freud onward, precipitating the passionate conviction that Jewish men and their images must change.

As Jewish men worked toward becoming bona fide Americans, Jewish women were increasingly pictured both as the repositories of Jewishness and as obstacles to Jewish men's achievement of their goals. Paula Hyman explains the dynamic: "Faced with the need to establish their own identities in societies in which they were both fully acculturated and yet perceived as partially Other because they were Jews, Jewish men were eager to distinguish themselves from the women of their community, whom they saw as the guardians of Jewishness. The negative representations of women that they produced reflected their own ambivalence about assimilation and its limits."[6]

Depending on the decade, Jewish women were portrayed as too loyal to tradition, too materialistic, or too selfish, or too controlling. Many films about Jews have depicted the struggle of Jewish men to acculturate and succeed in America. In the ethos of many such films, when Jewish men can successfully throw off the yoke of their women, they can enter unencumbered into mainstream white American life. Hollywood portrayals of Jewish women (which are usually created by Jewish men) are often reflections and vicarious reenactments of American Jewish men's rejection of their alien status, their projecting of that alien status onto Jewish women, or at the very least their unresolved relationship with their own ethnic and religious identities. Riv-Ellen Prell suggests that "the stereotypical suffocating mother or whiny and withholding wife express ideas about how Jewish men understand their own place in American society":

> These stereotypical women represent the anxiety, anger, and pain of Jewish men as they negotiate an American Jewish identity. Jewish women, in these

stereotypes, symbolize elements of "Jewishness" or "Americanness" to be rejected. Jewish women represent these features precisely because of their link to Jewish men, whom they do and do not resemble.[7]

The stereotypical portrayal of the putative Jewish American princess is shaped partially by internalized antisemitic images. At the same time, general American misogyny, a mistrust of bourgeois women that became widespread among American writers and intellectuals at mid-century, has played a very important role in the construction of negative images of the overbearing Jewish mother and the Jewish American princess as well.[8]

Significantly, the specifics of the princess image derive not from earlier Jewish stock characters but from American cultural and cinematic prescriptions for female deportment. As Jeanine Basinger notes, Hollywood films addressed women with "ambivalence" and "knowing pretense" as its films suggested "highly contradictory information" about women's lives: "Husbands were the most important thing in the world," but "men apparently were not to be trusted"; "Women were supposed to be sexually desirable, knowing how to tempt and satisfy men, but they were also supposed to be innocent and pure"; and, most of all,

> Women needed to be glamorous and lavishly dressed to gain the attention of men and the envy of other women (this latter being particularly important), but they were greedy little beasts if they coveted expensive clothes and jewelry. Instead of asking for things, they should create stunning outfits out of the draperies or produce a cookie jar crammed with about a million dollars' worth of egg money. . . .[9]

Jewish families increasingly became the repositories of once culture-wide critical pictures of the bourgeois family, with father as driven wage earner, mother as conspicuous consumer and guardian of the faith, and daughter as tender trap. Indeed, American Jewish ingénues in the late 1960s were increasingly described as demanding—rather than dissembling—"greedy little beasts." Jewish girls and women were portrayed in this voracious mode and cinematic portrayals defined by materialism. As Riv-Ellen Prell notes, Jewish literary and cinematic heroes "fled the triptych of Jewish life: hard work, personified by the father-producer; the creation of family, personified by the beautiful, sexual daughter; and the maintenance of Judaism, personified by the mother."[10]

Caricatures of Jews and Judaism as shallow and materialistic proliferated in novels and on screen and have profoundly influenced the way single Jews see each other, as our interview participants eloquently demonstrated in parts I and II of this book. Significantly, the same novels and films that satirize middle-class Jewish life often point to interfaith romance as a way to escape the oppressiveness of the Jewish family. Although one might suspect that these attitudes toward Jewish families are easing, the interview data suggest that these stereotypes have a very long shelf life.

During the post–World War II decades, when the American ethos of normalcy and family life yielded to widespread social change, Philip Roth and others highlighted the image of the Jewish male breaking free from Jewish bourgeois proprieties—and Jewish difference—by embracing a Christian woman. Especially beginning with the decade spanning the late 1960s and the late 1970s—an era of rapidly rising intermarriage rates—commercial Hollywood films increasingly pictured Jewish men gaining entrance to white American status through their romantic relationships with non-Jewish women.

Rather than being a "Good, Responsible & Dutiful" Jewish son, the enterprising "Jewboy" could take advantage of the astonishing discovery that "for every Eddie yearning for a Debbie, there is a Debbie yearning for an Eddie—a Marilyn Monroe yearning for her Arthur Miller"—a source of delight for the ambitious Jewish male, because "who in his right mind would ever have believed that Elizabeth Taylor had the hots for Uncle Hymie?" As Roth's Alexander Portnoy memorably complained:

> these blond-haired Christians are the legitimate residents and owners of this place.... O America! America! it may have been gold in the streets to my grandparents, it may have been a chicken in every pot to my father and mother, but to me, a child whose earliest movie memories are of Ann Rutherford and Alice Faye, America is a *shikse* nestling under your arm whispering love love love love love![11]

Although men were the signifying Jews in historical Jewish culture (and in most older antisemitic literature), women are increasingly portrayed as the signifying Jews in American films from the mid-twentieth century onward, bearing many of the stereotypical "Jewish" characteristics assigned by antisemitic literature. Jewish women thus serve as cultural decoys, while Jewish men are free to aspire to mainstream American status. Leaving the negative

"Jewish" characteristics to their mothers and sisters, Jewish men gain white American status through their romantic relationships with non-Jewish women, the gatekeepers to American society.

Perhaps nowhere is this principle more knowingly portrayed than in Woody Allen's 1978 masterpiece, *Annie Hall*. Allen's character, Alvy Singer, faces the viewer and announces that he can't stay married to Jewish women because they represent the Jewish "club" he won't join. Rejecting his Jewish ex-wives, Singer falls deeply in love with the epitome of the non-Jewish woman: long-legged, genetically blond, semi-incoherent Annie Hall, appealingly played by Diane Keaton. Like Roth's Alexander Portnoy, Alvy Singer both yearns after and derides white bread Christian America.

In a pivotal scene, Alvy Singer sits at Annie Hall's family dinner table in Chippewa Falls, Wisconsin, where they have gathered for Easter dinner over a "dynamite ham." Annie's tall, attractive, robust-looking family discusses swap meets and boat basins and friends with ludicrously stereotypical Christian names like "Randy Hunk." Alcohol takes precedence over food in their repast. Allen brings Alvy's own loudly argumentative, gluttonous, disease-obsessed family into the picture by creating a split screen. A conversation between the two families ensues; the Singers inform the Halls that during their holiday Jews fast for their sins. "What sins? I don't understand," puzzles the elegantly cool Mother Hall, leaving the Singers in consternation and confusion.

Not only are the Jews neurotic, even their religion, it seems, is neurotic. All of Alvy's attempts to match the coolness of Annie's family come to naught. As he sits at the table, Alvy feels old Grammie Hall staring at him with disgust. She sees him for what he is: a true Jew. In Grammie Hall's eyes, Alvy Singer is a bearded Hasidic Jew with flaming red, curly earlocks cascading down under his black hat.

Feminist film theory is a useful tool for unpacking the mythic power of the images in this scene. As Laura Mulvey explains, feminist film theory starts from Freud's definition of *scopophilia*, the pleasure of "a controlling and curious gaze," the action of looking that controls by reducing the other(s) to objects. Sitting in the darkened theater, the viewer gazes at the faces, forms, and actions of other people who cannot return the gaze. In a narrative film, the roles of men and women on the screen are divided: the lead male provides a heightened, ego-pleasurable "screen surrogate" with whom the viewer identifies. The lead woman, on the other hand, is presented as an erotically stylized object potentially available to the male protagonist—and through him, to the viewer. The lead male, often a policeman, lawyer, private eye, reporter, businessman, or intellectual, is always in a position to judge and control the eroticized female.[12] (Think of Alfred Hitchcock or later films such as *Dressed to Kill* (1980) and *L.A. Confidential* (1997).)

Identified minority figures seldom played these male leads until Woody Allen turned the tables. Although Jewish actors with non-Jewish names sometimes starred in films, their personas were usually deracinated and not identified as minorities. Roles for identified Jewish men—like roles for African American men—were usually auxiliary slots, included in order to carry a subtext or to provide a foil; in Rob Reiner's *A Few Good Men* (1992), for example, Kevin Pollak plays a Jewish assistant who bears the "Jewish" qualities of deep compassion and extreme caution, while the less "sensitive," more forceful—and gentile—Tom Cruise plays the male lead opposite Demi Moore.

Thus, when Woody Allen introduces a clearly and stereotypically ethnic Jewish male lead who pursues, judges, tries to save, and ultimately rejects the eroticized Annie Hall, the brilliance of the film arises partially from the ways in which Allen subverts the Hollywood formula. Allen seems to be "passing" as a romantic lead despite his hyperbolic Jewishness. But when Grammie Hall looks at Alvy and sees a bearded, black-frocked Hasid with long red earlocks, the elderly antisemite is religiously "outing" the Jew who dares to stand in narrative shoes that should be occupied by a real American.

Alvy Singer's discussion of his first Jewish wives, whom he rejects in favor of Annie Hall, sounds very similar to many of the real-life interviews reported in parts I and II of this study. In particular, Joel Millstein and Guy Naiman, each of whom saw their rejection of Jewish women as evidence of their rejection of oppressive Jewish proprieties, described their romances with non-Jewish women as symbolic of their independent thinking. In their narratives about their own lives, as well as in films about interfaith romance, Jewish men pursue non-Jewish women partly to express their values and goals. Some observers might wonder which came first, "the chicken or the egg"? In other words, have Jewish women and non-Jewish women become symbolic of tribal oppression versus individualistic freedom in real life, leading to this type of depiction in film, television, and popular culture, or have Jewish men come to see Jewish and non-Jewish women in this way because of the influence of the culture around them? One may well speculate that the influence goes in both directions. In any case, recent research reveals that these associations are widespread.

Querying Real People about the Media, Jews, and Gender

The Morning Star Commission in California (1997–1998) conducted discussions with diverse focus groups.[13] Participants, including men and women, Jews and non-Jews, were asked to pick out photos clipped from magazines and to talk about the "Jewish" or "non-Jewish" characteristics of the photos they had chosen. Their characterization of what it means to be Jewish or non-Jewish led to the follow hypotheses about the way contemporary Americans internalize cinematic images: (1) Media images of Jews, like literary and dramatic images of Jews, affect the social construction of reality. Audiences perceive certain characteristics as Jewish because they "know" from television, film, literature, and popular culture that these characteristics are found among Jews. Having "learned" that this is what Jews are like, they "see" Jews acting according to these characteristics in real life and the media. (2) Portrayals of Jews in the media produce and perpetuate stereotypical perceptions. Although film-makers, actors, and audiences may be unaware of the fact, the ways in which Jewish women and men are imaged on film echo European antisemitic stereotypes. (3) Jewish and non-Jewish Americans who watch television and film are absorbing stereotypical images of Jews. (4) Jewish femaleness is pictured as a kind of pathology, or at the very least an obstacle course for Jewish men. (5) When Jewish men absorb negative images of Jewish females, they may see Jewish women as unappealing, because they have learned from the media to interpret Jewish femaleness as unappealing.

The Morning Star Commission focus group discussions clearly indicated that media images shaped participants' perceptions. They had a clear impact on the way Jews are perceived and "Jewishness" is interpreted. Over and over again, both Jews and non-Jews described particular Jewish looks and behaviors. These putative signs of Jewishness were repeated in their descriptions of Jews in daily life and in the media. Semiotic indicators of Jewishness included (1) looking Jewish (noses and eyes); (2) sounding Jewish (voices); (3) acting Jewish (hysterical and domineering); (4) having Jewish attitudes toward money (men are stingy and women are compulsive consumers); (5) displaying Jewish modes of acquiring power (dominating and running things, lacking artistic creativity but buying creative influence with their vast funds).

Looking Jewish

Focus group participants were quite clear about the details of what it means to "look Jewish": the ubiquitous "big" Jewish nose, "heavy" features rather than "chiseled" features, large amounts of dark and curly hair, striking dark eyes (either large or squinted) with big eyebrows, short, buxom (for women), somewhat overweight, an appearance often accompanied by a kind of physical ineptitude. Several Jewish men made comments to the effect that Jewish women look like they have consumed "too many matza balls," and the image of sloppy, inelegant, undifferentiated roundness seemed to attach itself to the image of the women themselves.

Jewish women understood all too well that their own media images were usually not desirable. Among Jewishly affiliated women ages eighteen to thirty-four, perceptions of Jewish women on television were "outside of the mainstream of what is considered beautiful":

"They portray them as very educated, they're dorky, they're ugly."

"They're very serious."

"I'd definitely say that they're different."

"They're not glamorous."

Although most of the Jewish focus group participants insisted that Jewishness was a religion, not an ethnicity, clearly *looking Jewish takes Jewishness out of the category of religion and places it instead in the category of ethnicity, bordering on race.* The stereotypical elements of Jewish looks articulated by Jewish and non-Jewish respondents alike are reminiscent of the antisemitic assumptions about the "inferior type" of "Jewish-Negroid" features, as catalogued by Sander Gilman, that flourished among nineteenth-century non-Jewish intellectuals, writers, physicians, and communal officials.[14]

Because these "typical" Jewish looks identify a person as Jewish (and perhaps place one at a disadvantage) with or without individual choice, a hierarchy has developed in which Jews who do not look Jewish are perceived as being more desirable. Within this hierarchy, even a Jewish woman who is very beautiful cannot, by definition, be as desirable as a non-Jewish woman. As one male Jewish focus group participant struggled to explain this principle, it is "not to say that Jewish women are not beautiful, because they are . . . but they're not usually the tall, glamorous model types."

Hearing the Sounds of Jewish

Jewish identification can be assigned to characters not only because of the way they look, but perhaps even more so because of the way they sound, according to Morning Star Commission focus group participants. Over and over again, participants cited the "nasally" voice as a sure give-away for Jewish identity. Many Morning Star Commission focus group participants connected this nasal vocal quality to Jewish characters on television, especially Fran Drescher's characterization of "the Nanny," Franny Fine, whom they saw as being specifically Jewish, not just a New York ethnic. All of the focus groups, including those composed of Jewish women, insisted that Franny Fine–type Jewish women do not exist on television alone, and that they have encountered actual Jewish women who fit this image in real life.

Female focus group participants saw Jewish women on television as "them," a group with a distinctive sound:

"They talk a lot, Jewish women."

"Annoying."

"Very obnoxious."

"Nasal."

"It's not the normal—"

"It's her voice that makes her—"

Focus group participants detailed the way "annoying Jewish women" were in real life: "A lot of the Jewish girls I've met in high school have really been, like, dorky and annoying and nasally . . . they're right on TV sometimes, a lot of it." Jewish male participants also talked about the vocal quality of Jewish women: "Jewish women I've gone out with have been pretty loud and obnoxious and boisterous, which doesn't really bother me that much, because I tend to be the same way sometimes."

Poet Adrienne Rich remembers this hatred and fear of the sound of Jewish women's voices when she was growing up in the South as the daughter of a genteel Jewish father and a gentile mother. She, her sisters, and even her Christian mother internalized a belief in the essential Jewish voice and tried to make sure they never sounded Jewish:

With enough excellence, you could presumably make it stop mattering that you were Jewish; you could become the *only* Jew in the gentile world, a Jew so "civilized," so far from "common," so attractively combining southern gentility with European cultural values that no one would ever confuse you with the raw, "pushy" Jews of New York, the "loud, hysterical" refugees from eastern Europe, the "overdressed" Jews of the urban South. . . . I suppose that even my mother, pure gentile though she was, could be seen as acting "common" or "Jewish" if she laughed too loudly or spoke aggressively.[15]

Contemporary Jewish writer and publisher Daphne Merkin similarly recalled in *Esquire* that "Floating always among us was an awareness of the importance of avoiding, if one could help it, 'too Jewish' an appearance, the dread stigma of 'too Jewish' a voice."[16]

Worry about the Jewish voice betraying Jewish identity has a long history. Jewish languages were regarded with deep suspicion by European Christian clerics and peasants alike, who regarded them as hiding anti-Christian Jewish agendas and symbolizing the essential, ineluctable otherness of the Jew. Jewish accents were mocked in immigrant America at the turn of the century and in pre–World War II Germany. The Jew, with his or her unmistakable "hoarse, unmusical voice," was "never to be confounded with any other race."[17] In a world that now includes diverse Jewish public figures (with voices that differ greatly) such as Barbara Boxer, Diane Feinstein, Ruth Bader Ginsburg, Barbara Walters, and Melanie Mayron, one must wonder why the only Jewish women invoked by the focus group participants were those whom they claimed had "Jewish" voices: Barbra Streisand, Bette Midler, and, of course, "the Nanny," Fran Drescher, and her television mother and grandmother.

Acting Like a Jew

External environmental signals are perhaps most significant when it comes to perceiving what it means to "act like a Jew." Here there were important differences between the affiliated and unaffiliated Jews among the Morning Star Commission focus group participants. Jewish participants currently living in areas with Jewish population density, or who had grown up in Jewishly intensive environments, or who were highly affiliated at the current time, seemed less affected by media images. They displayed a vivid sense of the diversity of real Jewish personalities. For such affiliated Jews, being Jewish often had a concrete positive valence. One Jewish woman remembered Jewish familial warmth: "There was pride, there was something special about being Jewish . . . my grandfather was a rabbi and everything around the holidays was a real familial feeling."

However, even for these participants, Jewish self-denigration seems to live side by side with considerable self-esteem. Even the most positive, Jewishly aware women revealed their belief in the negative impact of certain "Jewish" characteristics. For example, one bright, attractive young woman who spoke eloquently about the intelligent, attractive, cultured, powerful Jewish women she had grown up with and still interacted with in real life also revealed a level of self-loathing when she admitted that she sometimes makes anti-Jewish jokes about herself. "If I catch myself doing something that reminds me of my parents, or my Czechoslovakian one-hundred-year-[old] nut-case grandmother I'll [say] *that's the Jew* [in me].

Acting like a Jew meant, to many focus group participants, being obsessed with money. Male and female, Jewish and non-Jewish, participants spontaneously reported frequently hearing the phrase "Jewing him down," meaning bargaining relentlessly for financial advantage. Some of the Jewish participants had heard "Jewing him down" used by acquaintances, business associates, friends, and non-Jewish inlaw relatives. Depending on how close they were to the person involved, many focus group participants were inclined to think that the person who said it had no antisemitic intent: "I know he doesn't really feel that way." Others were outraged by the same phrase.

Jewish male focus group participants at first tended to be rather cavalier about the impact of antisemitism in their lives. They tried to make light of stereotypes of Jews getting control of financial situations. Putting on a brave face, several suggested that these weren't such bad images. As one man laughingly put it, "We're rich and smart!" However, after they relaxed into the conversational dynamic of the focus groups, they shared, with evident sadness, pain, frustration, and anger, their feelings when they heard Jews described as cheap, physically inept, argumentative, overly anxious, or intellectual. They told stories in which Jewishness and stinginess had been linked in ways that degraded Jewish identity. Once the floodgates were opened, Jewish male participants spoke about insulting images that clearly cut to the bone: "I was in high school, hanging out with my ex-football teammates. There was a night, I believe at the local Edwards Theater, which it was $3.75 matinee night. They used to call it Jew night, playing up the stereotype that Jews were cheap." Another recalled, "I remember I was very uncomfortable and my fiancee was very uncomfortable. One time we were coming back from Vegas and we stopped at a truck stop in Lynwood . . . one of the truck drivers was being very discriminating against Jews, using that phrase and talking to the cashier at the store there, and she said something to him that he was being rude and stereotyping and perpetuating racism, and it made us feel very uncomfortable."

Non-Jewish participants also struggled with trying to figure out if phrases like "Jewing him down" were truly antisemitic or were just figures of speech. "Doesn't that mean being frugal? Isn't that a compliment?" suggested some participants.

But other non-Jewish participants were adamant that Jewish "frugalness" was evidence of their "stingy" nature. Words like "shyster" were used, although participants clearly had no sense of that phrase's ancestry in the character of Shakespeare's Shylock. One African American woman who grew up in Chicago placed Jewish stinginess into the context of Jewish family values. Jews, she asserted, teach their children to pursue and retain money at all costs, and they are especially careful to train their daughters to continue this behavior:

> They like to keep everything in the family. From the time a girl is small, five or six years old, they say, "Okay Madison, you're going to marry so and so and he's going to be an attorney when he grows up." And it's like they program them from a very small age to shoot for bucks. They will not allow, they will intercept in any way, if they think that a child is going to marry someone who they call commoner, or without money, that's a big issue with them.

Even when some participants in the group suggested that Jews were sometimes philanthropic, participants who perceived Jews as being obsessed with money insisted that Jews always have an angle: if Jews are philanthropic, it is because they think they will get something out of it.

This conviction that Jews are stingy has a long history in European antisemitic images of the Jew as usurious moneylender, immortalized in the aforementioned character of Shylock. In Philip Roth's novel *Operation Shy-*

lock: A Confession, a scholar of Yiddish literature named Supposenik holds forth on the undestructablity of this ugly stereotype of the Jew:

> I studied those three words by which the savage, repellent, and villainous Jew, deformed by hatred and revenge, entered as our doppleganger into the consciousness of the enlightened West. Three words encompassing all that is hateful in the Jew, three words that have stigmatized the Jew through two Christian millennia and that determine the Jewish fate until this very day. . . . You remember Shylock's opening line? You remember the three words? What Jew can forget them? What Christian can forgive them? *Three thousand ducats.* . . . The hateful, hateful Jew whose artistic roots extend back to the Crucifixion pageants at York, whose endurance as the villain of history no less than of drama is unparalleled, the hook-nosed moneylender, the miserly, money maddened, egotistical degenerate . . . this is Europe's Jew, the Jew expelled in 1290 by the English, the Jew banished in 1492 by the Spanish, the Jew terrorized by Poles, butchered by Russians, incinerated by Germans, spurned by the British and the Americans while the furnace roared at Treblinka.[18]

Equally significant, the image of Jews as stingy and self-absorbed is absolutely the opposite of the way in which most American Jews perceive themselves. Non-Jewish participants frequently used the word "conservative" to describe pictures of Jews, by which they often meant careful, cautious, or conservative about money. When American Jews described themselves, however, they often equated Jewish identity with liberalism and generosity. In the 1997 *Annual Survey of American Jewish Public Opinion* conducted for the American Jewish Committee by Market Facts, Inc., only 26 percent of respondents said they were "slightly conservative," "conservative," or "extremely conservative." Not surprisingly, 76 percent said they had voted for Bill Clinton in the 1996 presidential election. The respondents in this poll, as in other polls of Jewish opinion, strongly supported legalized abortion and a generous immigration policy, and they rejected the view that equal rights have been pushed too far in the United States, feeling instead that special consideration in hiring and promotion for disadvantaged minorities was still justified.[19] The gap between the demonstrable attitudes of actual American Jews and some antisemitic images of American Jews is particularly striking.

Another commonly mentioned aspect of "acting like a Jew" devolved around shrill or hysterical behavior. Participants found this quality in both men and women, although it was mentioned more frequently with regard to women. Yet another related aspect of "acting like a Jew" was "domineering" or "manipulative" behavior. Jewish women were described as "always riding their husbands" by non-Jewish female participants. The combination of "hysterical" and "domineering and manipulative" behavior can, of course, be easily found in films, most notably Mel Brooks's *The Producers,* which hilariously defines both the hysterical—Gene Wilder—and the manipulative—Zero Mostel—Jewish males. The list of Jewish women in television and film who fit these stereotypes is lengthy, but the Mike Meyers's *Saturday Night Live* "Coffee Klatch" lady, Linda Richmond, who gave audiences discussion topics when she feels *farklempt,* would fit the bill.

The Jewish Woman as Upper-Middle-Class Consumer

In my interview research, I repeatedly heard Jewish homes described as materialistic and especially Jewish women pilloried as voracious consumers. Some of these conversations are reported in part I of this book, as when Guy Naiman discussed his materialistic Jewish wife and her controlling parents. In the Morning Star Commission focus groups, Jewish women were also repeatedly identified as conspicuous consumers by participants. Their careless hunger for and obsession with material objects was often tied into their manipulativeness. Among the Jewish female participants, stereotypes of Jewish women as materialistic consumers had been deeply internalized. Many expressed these images with a kind of cartoon like directness:

> "She's probably very Jappie. She probably likes to shop at Barneys and Saks, Neiman Marcus and Nordstroms. Nordstroms isn't even good enough for her."
> "Jewish women, even the way Jewish men see them is that they want to marry somebody to support them. They don't want to work. But somebody who is not Jewish, she's going to make a good wife and she don't care about money, but Jewish women, all they want is nice clothes and nice rings."

They also permeated the messages many women remembered about growing up Jewish:

> "You were supposed to marry a nice Jewish boy."
> "Rich boy. Lawyer, doctor, accountant."

"At my house it was no chuppy, no shtuppy" [no marriage canopy, no sexual relations—Yiddish slang].

These negative self-images of materialistic, middle-class Jews have been a cornerstone of acceptable antisemitism from the time that Jews entered the middle classes after emancipation. Jews have repeatedly been singled out for moving economically in exactly the way their emancipators hoped they would. In novels, D. H. Lawrence noted with revulsion "the prosperous Jews," Edith Wharton made marrying a rich Jew only one step above prostitution for her genteel but impoverished heroine, and F. Scott Fitzgerald placed aggressive, monied Jews on the fringes of established society. In all of these cases, Jewish men, rather than women, suffered from negative portrayals when they used money to become part of upper-class society.

A related antisemitic belief is that Jews acquire excellence either by working very hard for it or by purchasing it. Nineteenth-century thinkers and ordinary men were frequently convinced of this, and the stereotype of Jewish success only coming through vulgar striving or money is brilliantly captured in the film *Chariots of Fire,* in which a dazzlingly fast—and strikingly semitic—track-racing competitor is scorned by the administrators of his English school because he is the "typical . . . son of a tradesman" who "tries too hard."

In contrast, in American television programs and films of the past few decades it is usually Jewish women rather than Jewish men who obtain a desirable veneer through money and effort. Films written, directed, and/or produced by Jewish men often transfer the negative attention on Jewish upward socioeconomic mobility away from themselves and onto Jewish women. Thus, many Americans have absorbed the impact of images such as the well-dressed figures of Natalie Wood's "Shirley" in *Marjorie Morningstar* (1959), Ali McGraw's plumbing heiress Brenda Patimkin in *Goodbye, Columbus* (1968), Goldie Hawn's spoiled "princess" Judy who becomes *Private Benjamin* (1985), Bette Midler's hyphenated pseudo-intellectual professional who replaces personal relationships with a passion for material possessions in *Scenes from a Mall* (1991), and numerous others. Non-Jewish women can be effortlessly attractive in a non-flashy, non-vulgar way, in the words of one Morning Star Commission focus group participant: "That whole delicate kind of features, not like gorgeous, but kind of pretty and kind of clean, and very nicely dressed, conservative." However, beauty does not come naturally to Jewish women—they must buy it. Gilda Radner's famous *Saturday Night Live* stint as a tongue-in-cheek advertising icon, "The Jewess in Jewish Jeans," and the materialistic three-generation matriarchy in *The Nanny* are only the latest in a long line of Jewish women who live to spend, who love to shop, and who always look marvelous.

Jewish Women and Men Perceive Themselves and Each Other

One of the most intriguing aspects of the Morning Star Commission focus group discussions was the way in which the Jewish participants described the photographs they themselves had chosen as "typical" Jews. Men described their chosen Jewish men as embodying several well-known but believable types: (1) The liberal schlemiel: "From the clothes he is or isn't wealthy, he's probably not real wealthy, although I should talk. He's probably never been married. I would say he's a teacher, and if there's picketing he's probably there." (2) The *macher*-on-the-make (A *macher* is an Americanized Yiddish expression for a communal "big shot.") who is a closet mama's boy: "I think he's a student at N.Y.U. . . . and studying to be a stockbroker or something. . . . He's conservative [but] he's got a little wild streak in him, that's why he's got a five o'clock shadow going. He looks like he's kind of a mama's boy, so he probably has a very Jewish mother, always 'Eat your chicken soup.' I think he's probably a lifelong bachelor." (3) The intellectual and independent spirit: "He's a writer. I think he was really shy and confused when he was a child, but now that he's kind of on his own and does his own thing . . . he found out who he is. I think he likes the rain . . . he has a jagged sense of humor, but I think he's really sincere, and sensitive too." (4) The Jewy Jew: "He's had a very religious upbringing, might even have spoken Yiddish as a first language. He grew up in New York, or definitely the East Coast. He's a very sweet man, he's a family man. He has a kind of nasally voice. He likes to talk with his hands. He is a very modest man but he's very educated. He's also a spokesman for Jewish causes, Jewish community, and he takes that responsibility very seriously." Interestingly enough, only female participants mentioned two stereotypes that are quite prevalent in media portrayals of Jewish men: (5) The hustler/shark who steps on anyone to get where he needs to go (see Philip Roth's Mr. Patimkin and Richler's Duddy Kravitz for examples of this type); and (6) the pathetic wimp, consumed by anxiety (take your pick from roles by Gene Wilder and Woody Allen).

When it came to describing typical Jewish women, Jewish men tended less to specifics and more toward generalities. Jewish men tended to divide Jewish women into archetypical categories: (1) Yiddeshe mamas: nurturing older women who know how to make "killer chicken soup" and care deeply and perhaps obsessively about others: "This is Sophie, sitting here with her husband of thirty-five years. . . . She's never worked outside the house. She got married at the age of twenty. Her idea of exercise is hand to mouth. She'll die early because she is probably a little overweight. She's a great cook. High school degree, that's it. Wouldn't hurt a fly. Has lots of knickknacks in the house. If her husband dies, she will never get remarried." (2) Americanized Jewish princesses: "Trendy. When it's Farrah's hair, they've got Farrah's hair. When it's Jennifer Aniston's hair, they've got Jennifer Aniston's hair. Whoever is in, they got the clothes. They follow pop culture." (3) Career viragos, Jewish women who are driven and ambitious and not particularly people-oriented, often younger women who "know what they want" and "don't take any guff from anyone." (4) Nice Jewish good girls, seemingly sweet, ordinary, responsible Jewish women of varying ages.

Influenced by these negative images of each other, the singles among the Morning Star Commission Jewish focus group participants often did not find themselves attracted to Jews of the opposite sex. Among the affiliated Jewish women ages eighteen to thirty-four, three women talked about their dating patterns:

"I don't date Jewish men. My mother has a real problem with it, my family does. For some reason, I don't do it on purpose, but I don't wind up attracted to them."

"Same exact thing with me."

"I'm turned off by Jewish guys. They're so anal retentive, I swear."

Choosing to Be Perceived as Jewish

With such common negative perceptions of Jewish identity, it is not surprising that Morning Star Commission Jewish focus group participants talked about picking and choosing the situations when they wanted to be perceived as Jews. As Mary Waters points out, "people have more and more latitude about how to self-identify and whether to do so in ethnic terms." Increasingly permeable boundaries in contemporary American society make ethnic identification a matter of choice for white Americans. Whether or not—and when—individuals choose to identify themselves as belonging to a particular ethnic group often depends on whether such identification is rewarded or punished by the people around them. Thus, some Americans perceive that "in contrast to families for whom there seem to be positive benefits in enhancing an ethnic identity—for example by calling themselves Irish, Italian, or Polish . . . there are negative social costs associated respectively with labeling children Jewish or Hispanic."[20]

The Morning Star Commission focus group data clearly illustrate the impact of environment on whether or not an individual chooses to be identified as a Jew. Jews who have grown up and/or currently live or work in largely non-Jewish environments perceive the outside world as being antisemitic. This perception of hostile surroundings makes them feel that they will be jeopardizing themselves in some way if they identify themselves as Jews. For some participants, like this Jewish male, the association of Jewishness with unpleasant sensations of *difference* began with childhood:

> I generally went to schools where there were very few Jewish students, so it was tough. I felt different, a minority, and the Christmas season was tough, because of singing Christmas carols and Christmas trees. When I was asked to talk a little about Hanukkah, I guess I had mixed emotions. One, it put some attention on me, which was kind of interesting. Everybody was asking me questions about it. On the other hand, I felt different.

Focus group participants were clearest about the negative impact of an antisemitic environment when it came from strangers. Many of the stories they told about being subjected to verbal slurs occurred in situations in which they were not on their home turf—they were traveling or participating in an unusual activity that brought them into contact with people they didn't know. One Jewish female participant in the age eighteen to thirty-four group told about the special vulnerability one feels in this kind of situation: "I was a youth group organizer for a Jewish organization, and we took all the kids to the World Wrestling. . . . Here we were, a bunch of little Jewish kids, and a couple of counselors. They found out we were Jewish. Some of the remarks that were coming out of their mouths . . . I should have said something, but I didn't feel safe." Within this perception of a hostile environment, any stranger is potentially an antisemite, and unfamiliarity signals danger.

However, many Morning Star Commission focus group participants also told stories about verbal slurs coming from friends or inlaw family members. These comments created a type of cognitive dissonance: on one hand, they didn't like the things that were said, but on the other hand, they couldn't accept that people whom they wanted to like them were saying unpleasant things to them. The most common response to this cognitive dissonance was to explain it away by assuming that friends and family didn't—couldn't—really mean what they were saying. The same comments signaled hostility from a stranger but didn't really mean anything when uttered by a friend. One Jewish woman in the age eighteen to thirty-four group tried to explain how she differentiated between the actual racism of her boyfriend's sixty-seven-year-old father and her "friends," who are "just kids." About the boyfriend's father, she said, "He called me a heathen one time. . . . One time I kept peering into the house because I kept ringing the doorbell and I couldn't see. I was looking to see if anyone was home. He's like, 'I thought there was a little Jew peering into my house.' He was just awful. He made nose faces when someone is cheap. . . ." A listening participant agreed, "If is comes from your friends, and they know it's not true, but they're just messing around," comments were not offensive. Another Jewish woman in the age eighteen to thirty-four group first claimed that she has never experienced any hostile comments about being Jewish but then recalled her non-Jewish mother-in-law's words: "My mother-in-law once said to me, 'He Jewed her down.' I looked at her and I couldn't believe my mother-in-law said that to me. I don't feel that they're racist people."

Because negative feelings about Jews can be expressed by friends and strangers alike, *not* looking like a Jew becomes a protective device. For many, a non-Jewish appearance places one into a different category of Jew—the Jew who can pass—and is experienced as a badge of honor. This is especially true for Jewish women. To be a Jewish woman who doesn't look Jewish is to belong to a superior caste.

An individual may be inadvertently identified as Jewish by others if he or she (1) has a distinctive Jewish name, or (2) "looks Jewish." If either one of these conditions apply, choice is taken away from the individual, who can no longer choose whether or not to identify as a Jew. Looking Jewish diminishes personal autonomy, one of the most cherished conditions of American life, and can even be perceived as diminishing the individual's status as an American.

Even Steven: Interfaith Families as a Cultural Ideal

Within the past two decades interfaith families and dual religious observances have come to be presented as a cultural ideal in television programming for children as well as adults. The media promote mixed marriage, and religious syncretism in mixed-married households. Readers who watch television can probably supply their own list of examples from numerous popular series such as *Thirtysomething*, in which a Jewish husband and his Christian wife perform acts of religious generosity that echo O'Henry's "The Gift of the Magi": the husband facilitates his wife having a Christmas tree, which he previously had opposed, and she polishes his menorah in preparation for Hanukkah, which she had previously ignored. Thus, they are united in marital loving kindness in the celebration of each other's religious traditions.

One Nickelodeon program for children, *As Told by Ginger* (December 2, 2002), is also particularly revealing. Ginger, the protagonist, discovers that she has Jewish as well as Christian ancestry. She is confused about how to honor her Jewish antecedents. At first, she refuses to participate in any Christmas festivities, because she wishes "to be fair to my Jewish heritage." However, she then feels she is not being "fair to my Christian heritage." In the end, Ginger decides to include both Jewish and Christian symbols into her December life. Surrounded by colorful accoutrements such as a Christmas tree, hanging stockings, and a menorah, Ginger, her mother, and her friends joyfully celebrate her "even Steven" solution to her double religions.

With current programming, only occasionally does one encounter a Jewish man married to a Jewish woman, as in the November 2002 wedding of Debra Messing to a Jewish doctor in *Will and Grace*. Aside from historical dramatizations (i.e., *Brooklyn Bridge*), mixed marriage is ubiquitous. Religious syncretism is presented as appropriate behavior in Jewish-Christian households, a symbol of American empathy and religious tolerance. Within the cultural artifacts that help to shape American understandings of what is real and good, two-religion households have been normalized and are presented as a new cultural ideal.

The impact of these cultural celebrations of religious syncretism can be observed in the real life stories of our informants. For example, the Jewish mother who insisted on taking her Jewish-raised children to candlelight church services so that they could honor their father's Christian traditions echoes the inclusivist moral vision of Nickelodeon's *As Told by Ginger*.

At the same time, it is very possible that antisemitic images of Jews are declining. Younger Americans, Jews and non-Jews alike, may indeed have far less ethnic, urban, or stereotypical notions of what Jewish men and women are like. And perhaps, paradoxically, it will be the very presence of so many Jews in Christian families that will lessen the salience of these old and in many ways unrealistic ways of seeing, hearing, and interpreting Jewish characters and real Jews.

9

MIXED MESSAGES ARE THE MEDIUM

The mixed-married Jewish community has grown, and, as we have seen, is regarded as normative in the broader general American culture. Within Jewish communal settings as well, the increasing prominence of mixed-married households has precipitated re-evaluations of long-held attitudes and policies. Whereas mixed marriage was historically discouraged within all wings of Judaism, today negative statements about intermarriage have measurably declined. Indeed, several groups, such as the secular Jewish humanists, the Reform movement, and Jewish communal organizations with their "neutral turf" each have declared themselves as ideally positioned to understand and meet the needs of mixed-married families. Each of these groups asserts that they have special expertise in dealing with mixed-married families, and thus are the natural leaders for the wave of the future. However, many spokespersons for these groups seem loathe to face the future without finding precedents from the past. Much of the liberal literature exhibits a fascinating determination to base innovative strategies on interpretations of Jewish history and texts that seem to support religious pluralism, tolerance, and inclusiveness.

Secular, Religious, and Communal Responses

Secularism has increased within Jewish communities around the world, and is especially pronounced in the mixed-married population. Many mixed-married couples opt to raise their children as "no religion," or in something that they call "both, but secular-cultural, not religious." They are supported in this lifestyle choice by books, websites, and other materials produced by the secular Jewish humanist movement and others who promote a secular approach to Jewish identification. However, it should be noted that although many more Jews today than in past decades call themselves "secular," in the United States secular Jewish movements often have some sort of an attachment to religion and do not, as individuals do in Europe and Israel, simply eschew religion. Rather, American Jewish secularism as a movement tends toward the reinterpretation of religious ideas and activities through a nontheistic lens.

Bonnie Cousens, the executive director of the Society for Humanistic Judaism in Michigan, suggests that humanistic Jews "believe very strongly that it is important to serve intermarried families; because of our openness, we are attractive to many intermarried families,"[21] As Judy Petsonk and Jim Remsen, authors of *The Intermarriage Handbook,* explain, "the decades since the 1960s have been a time of questioning, excitement, and spiritual search in America. There has been a great deal of experimentation with native religions, Eastern religions and meditation," and even mainstream Protestant denominations, influenced by "feminists and committed social activists," have experimented with "liturgy, social action, and new forms of organization." These trends have been equally significant in American Jewish societies. An important influence in this secular-religious experimentation is humanism, because

> the humanistic religious option has been a boon to intermarried couples who are looking for a comfortable common ground. Humanistic religious communities . . . do not demand obedience and they respect freedom of conscience. Instead of emphasizing the risk of sin, they stress the possibility that people can achieve their full potential; instead of instilling guilt, they try to inspire creativity and hope. Christian humanists emphasize Jesus as a man and teacher. Jewish humanists, such as those in Reform and Reconstructionism, encourage lay participation and see religion as a rich treasury of human experience rather than a set of divine commands.[22]

Responses to the intermarried population, of course, come from within the mainstream Jewish movements as well. The initiatives of the Reform movement are especially important because, although exogamy has transformed all of American Jewish life, the Reform movement has been most affected by rising numbers of Jews marrying out. This is partially because more raised-Reform Jews have married non-Jews, but even more so because of self-selection: Jews raised in Orthodox or Conservative milieus often join Reform congregations—or at least start to describe themselves as Reform—after they marry non-Jews. Because the Reform movement is widely perceived to be more "flexible" in its relationship to *halakhah* (rabbinic law), and has in fact historically defined itself as not bound by rabbinic Judaism, many mixed-married Jews assume that they, their non-Jewish spouses, and their children would be more welcome in Reform congregations.

As a result, Reform congregations include by far the largest proportion of Jews who are married to non-Jews or are parents of adult children involved in mixed marriages. The leadership of the Reform movement has struggled for decades to define the movement's official stance toward this increasingly significant client group. The response of Reform rabbis and lay leaders has been far from monolithic. Thus, although the umbrella organization of Reform rabbis, the Central Conference of American Rabbis (CCAR), passed a resolution in 1973 urging that its members "desist from officiating at mixed marriages," a substantial and probably growing group of Reform rabbis continued to perform marriages between Jews and non-Jews.[23]

Rabbis who perform mixed marriages often see themselves as the only realists among their religious colleagues. They argue that they and they alone are holding the door open for Jewish development in the families that will be raised by the couples they marry. Many of the rabbis who have performed mixed marriages over the past few decades report that they do so on the principle that a rabbinic presence at the marriage fosters more Jewish identification within the household itself. Some rabbis insist that the children be raised as Jews in order for them to officiate at a mixed marriage. Others make no such stipulation, noting that more conversions take place after marriage than before. Since non-Jews are sometimes moved to convert into Judaism when children are born, begin their Jewish schooling, and approach their bar/bat mitzvah celebrations, rabbis who marry mixed couples feel that they are taking the first step in moving the family along a Jewish road. Moreover, they make the point that conversion itself is only one chapter in the developmental process of becoming a Jew.

Among those who perform mixed marriage, some are willing to perform in concert with a priest or Christian clergyman and some are not. As we have seen (chapter 3), mixed-married couples often communicated the names of the various types of rabbis who perform mixed marriage through a kind of underground railroad.

As of 1995, slightly under half of the Reform rabbis who belong to the CCAR (48 percent) reported that they performed mixed-marriage ceremonies, as did 38 percent of members of the Reconstructionist Rabbinical Association of America.[24] Current estimates put the proportion of Reform and Reconstructionist rabbis now officiating at mixed marriage as higher than these figures indicate. Those rabbis who refuse to perform mixed marriages often find that their resistance is perceived with hostility by mixed-marrying couples and their children. Rabbis who point out that the Jewish wedding contract stipulates a marriage "according to the laws of Moses and Israel"—but who are anxious to draw the newlywed couple into their congregations after the wedding has been performed by someone else—are often bitterly described as "hypocritical" by the families involved.[25] The approach these rabbis use is mandated by rabbinic law. However, since Reform rabbis are perceived to have more freedom of choice, and the Reform movement has long since distanced itself from the authority of rabbinic law, perhaps the halakhic argument is unconvincing to distraught parents and angry children.

As the numbers of mixed-married households associated with Reform Judaism grew exponentially in the 1970s and 1980s, pressure on the Reform movement increased commensurately to accommodate this new population in some meaningful way. The CCAR issued a patrilineal descent decision in 1983, stating that "the child of one Jewish parent is under the presumption of Jewish descent," with the child's acceptance of Jewish identity later "established through appropriate and timely public and formal acts of identification with the Jewish faith and people."[26]

The patrilineal descent decision fits in with an ideological category of changes championed by Reform Judaism: the erasure of hierarchies among the Jewish people. Historical Jewish societies were stratified into numerous hierarchies, including gender hierarchies. Today, many American Jews believe that religiously based social inequality is unacceptable, even repugnant. The Reform patrilineal descent declaration changed the millenia-old Jewish practice of considering the mother's religion as the defining factor in the religion of her children. Under this new dispensation, either the father's or the mother's Jewishness could be the basis for a child's status as Jewish, provided that the child declared the intent to be Jewish once he or she had reached an appropriate age. Many Reform leaders presented the patrilineal descent decision as a victory for morality and egalitarianism. Now Jewish men and Jewish women would be treated equally under Reform Jewish law. What the patrilineal descent decision meant in practical terms is that non-Jewish wives do not need to convert before children are born in order for those children to be considered Jewish.

Sociologically, the acceptance of the patrilineal descent decision has had two unintended consequences. First, as we have seen, Jewish women are often portrayed in very unflattering terms in American fiction, film, television, and popular culture (chapter 8). As long as matrilineal descent was the unifying principle of all of the American wings of Judaism—as it is in Jewish communities worldwide—Jewish women enjoyed a "market advantage" in marriage that to some extent offset the very real handicaps they suffered because of ubiquitous negative stereotypes. With the erasure of the matrilineal descent principle in Reform Judaism, Jewish women lost the advantage that only they could produce Jewish children. There was no longer any need for a Jewish man to marry a Jewish woman, or to urge his non-Jewish spouse to convert into Judaism.

Second, a higher ratio of non-Jewish mothers is linked to a lower ratio of Jewish attachments within mixed-married homes. Despite the optimism of the patrilineal descent decision, every systematic study of the Jewish community has shown that Jewish mothers provide more intensive and extensive connections to Jews and Judaism than do Jewish fathers in mixed-married households. Whether the measure is cultural, institutional, social, or religious, having a Jewish mother in the household (born or converted) makes the households far more likely to incorporate Jewish activities and values.

The Reform movement has taken the lead in creating and implementing diverse initiatives designed to bring mixed-married couples and their families closer to Judaism. Some of these programs operate through Reform temples; others are situated within community settings. Many of these programs have in common a very gentle approach, sensitive to the conflicts and multiple needs of the mixed-married family. These programs are accompanied by a series of publications. Some of them deal directly with the issue of mixed marriage. Recently, online "publications" have become most prevalent: *Intermarried? Reform Judaism Welcomes You; Inviting Someone You Love to Become a Jew; When a Family Member Converts: Questions and Answers About Conversion to Judaism.*[27] Other publications include syllabi and self-help books on how to create Jewish connections in a mixed-married home. For example, an attractive primer on Jewish observance, *A Taste of Judaism,* walks families who may be unsure about how to navigate the Jewish calendar through many presumably enjoyable observances.

According to Dru Greenwood, for many years director of outreach for the Reform movement and herself a Jew by choice, the goal of Reform outreach to the mixed-married community has always been and continues to be the willing and joyous conversion of the non-Jewish spouse. The movement seeks to avoid coercion toward conversion, on one hand, and religious syncretism, on the other hand. Thus, Reform outreach efforts never pressure non-Jewish spouses to convert. At the same time, the Reform movement has a principle that children who are simultaneously being given formal church education and formal Jewish education will not be accepted into Reform congregational religious schools. Many administrators note, however, that they often don't ask about dual schooling, and few attempts are made to ensure it once a child is accepted into a school.

Mushrooming numbers of mixed-married households have created a new demographic. Not surprisingly, their presence has generated responses not only within the movements of American Judaism but also outside them. Some responses are entrepreneurial, a veritable mixed-marriage industry. From Internet chat rooms to scores of self-help books to greeting cards specially geared to the ever-expanding mixed-married client group, mixed marriage has become big business. Popular publications urging the most inclusive approach to mixed marriage have proliferated. A very small sampling includes *The Half-Jewish Book: A Celebration; The Intermarriage Handbook: A Guide for Jews and Christians; The Interfaith Family Guidebook: Practical Advice for Jewish and Christian Partners,* and a new guide for interfaith romances, *What To Do When You're Dating a Jew: Everything You Need to Know from Matza Balls to Marriage.*[28] The *Forward* quoted Egon Mayer, director of the Center for Jewish Studies of the Graduate Center of the City University of New York, as follows: "*What To Do When You're Dating a Jew* makes 'an important contribution to what's needed out there.' Being for or against intermarriage 'is like being for or against the weather,' he said. 'It's a demographic and social reality.' (*Forward* online, November 16, 2000).

The inclusiveness and outreach approach, perhaps most consistently voiced by the publications of the Jewish Outreach Institute (JOI), cites the large percentage of mixed marriages revealed by the 1990 NJPS to insist that mixed marriage is an inevitable consequence of the contemporary open

American society. In a JOI pamphlet written by Jewish communal leader David G. Sacks, for example, readers are told that mixed marriage is a phenomenon as fixed and unavoidable as "cycles of the sun and the tides."[29] In speaking of the children of mixed marriage, the JOI pamphlet asserts that "they are all Jewish to some degree," but does not indicate that they are also frequently *not* Jewish to some degree. In keeping with the American attitude that any parental interference is best administered with a very light touch, some of the outreach literature warns parents to show the utmost delicacy. Young Jews involved in exogamous relationships are portrayed as fragile and naïve, in the most romantic possible light:

> Parents of the intermarried need to take special care not to "poison" the natural openness of the young couple to family history by openly or subtly emphasizing the young couple's curiosity about family history through the sharing of stories that invite admiration, empathy, and emulation. . . . Open to them the treasure trove of your own family memories, be it in conversations or letters. These may well be the first heirlooms with which they will "Judaize" their own new nest.[30]

According to this approach, having Jewish ancestors is similar to other white European ethnic derivations, as described by Mary Waters: ethnic white Americans "do not give much attention to the ease with which they are able to slip in and out of their ethnic roles. It is natural to them that in the greater part of their lives, their ethnicity does not matter."[31] In this light-hearted approach, being Jewish carries no serious historical weight or meaning. These familial pregenerators are potential sources for warm, fuzzy echoes from the past, but they have no impact on familial commitments and destiny.

In yet another approach to incorporating non-Jewish partners into Jewish families and communities, Israel Minister of Justice Yossi Beilin has called for secular conversion. Beilin, who published a book on the subject, explains that such converts would be joining "the Jewish people, which is not necessarily based on the Jewish religion."[32] In Israel, secular Jewish converts speak Hebrew, serve in the Israeli army, and participate in the nonreligious culture-wide celebrations of the Jewish holidays throughout the year, as well as participate in Israeli patriotic commemorations such as Yom Yerushalayim (Jerusalem Day), Yom HaZikaron (IDF fallen soldiers remembrance day), and Yom HaAtzmaut (Israeli Independence Day). Thus, a secular conversion to Jewishness in Israel means extensive involvement in Jewish socio-political destiny as well as Jewish cultural activities. Absent this secular Jewish cultural environment, however, it is not clear how a secular conversion would be supported and reinforced in the United States, especially given Steven M. Cohen's argument that for younger American Jews ethnicity has largely lost its salience, and Jewishness is perceived as religious identification.[33] Beilin's proposal may be an unwitting illustration of the experiential gap that exists between the conditions of Jewish life in Israel and the Diaspora.

Finding a Usable Past

Responses to the phenomenon of mixed marriage not only provide a fascinating lens through which to view trends in American Jewish religious and communal movements, but also reveal a particularly compelling illustration of a sociological phenomenon that I call "coalescence." During the process of coalescence the texts of two cultures, American and Jewish, are accessed simultaneously, much as one might access two different texts on a single computer screen. These value systems coalesce or merge, and the resulting merged messages are perceived not as being American and Jewish values side by side but as being a unified text, which is identified as normative Judaism.

Leaders and policy planners suggesting strategies for dealing with contemporary mixed-married families, while they argue for modern approaches, often search for proof texts about historical Jewish behaviors to support their arguments. Their task is to find a usable past—that is, a past that seems to provide precedents or foundations for the strategies they propose to deal with current circumstances. Innovative strategies are presented as having sacred, ancient roots. Coalescence is especially evident in the vocabulary employed by activists within the various outreach organizations, who present historical Judaism—especially biblical Judaism—as "inclusive" in its approach to non-Jews.

To cite just two examples, Rabbis Kerry M. Olitzky and Barbara Rosman Penzer use biblical injunctions and narratives to support more inclusive outreach efforts. Olitzky, executive director of the JOI, declares that "the idea of welcoming and loving the stranger is so basic to the formation of the Jewish religious psyche that it is emphasized even more frequently than are the laws of Shabbat or the laws of *kashrut*." Olitzky points out that instructions on loving the stranger are "repeated over 30 times, in various combinations, throughout the Torah, reiterated more often than any other commandment."[34]

Similarly, Penzer suggests that biblical figures illustrate the normalcy, indeed the desirability, of incorporating unconverted non-Jews, whether they be "a lapsed Catholic, or a non-church-goer, or an active member of your church," into Jewish households and the Jewish people:

> Welcome, fellow-traveler. You join a long line of venerated women, including Tzipporah, the wife of Moses, and Asenat, the wife of Joseph and mother of Menasseh and Ephraim, whose names are invoked in the blessing for our sons in the *Shabbat* (the Jewish Sabbath) evening ritual. These women receive little attention in our tradition, certainly less than Ruth, who is known for her choice to join the Jewish people. Yet, they raised up leaders for the Jewish people. . . .[35]

Passages such as these coalesce contemporary Western ideas such as inclusiveness with ancient concepts, such as being kind to the "righteous convert" [*ger tzedek*, often rendered as "stranger"]. In the resulting mix, biblical Israelites are portrayed as interacting warmly with their non-Israelite neighbors and spouses. This depiction has enormous emotional and intellectual resonance for many American Jews. The blurring of boundaries between insider and outsider, creating the image of a biblical inclusivist utopia, reflects the fact that American Jews like to think of Judaism as a faith tradition that encourages inclusiveness. Arguably, American Jews yearn to think of themselves as inclusive—and included!—because so much of historical Jewish experience has been marked by exclusiveness. Sociologists have noted that the enduring American Jewish sense of vulnerability is linked to the anxiety that Jews may still be singled out for discrimination or persecution.

The particularly American nature of this Judaism-as-inclusiveness construct is especially evident when examined in light of Jewish and Christian scholarship suggesting that biblical, ancient, and medieval Jewish societies each had strongly defined boundaries between insiders and outsiders, although they shifted over time. Given the power and salience of the current coalesced image of an inclusive Judaism, some attention to historical trajectories is in order. Harvard University historian Shaye Cohen, for example, demonstrates that biblical Judaism did not obliterate the status demarcations between Israelite and resident stranger. Non-Jewish "mixed multitudes" and "resident aliens" that attached themselves to the people of Israel occupied a different status than the Israelite or Judean population, remaining distinct and not blending into Jewish families and societies, although Jewish laws protected them from exploitation.[36]

Interestingly, the Sabbath laws were one of the vehicles for prescribing social responsibility within a hierarchical structure. While ancient Israelite society was highly structured, the intensely regulated "holy rest" of the Sabbath imposed a kind of "social equality" upon all layers of society, argues writer Judith Shulevitz in the *New York Times Magazine:*

> The Israelite Sabbath institutionalized an astonishing, hitherto undreamed of notion: that every single creature has the right to rest, not just the rich and privileged. Covered under the Fourth Commandment are women, slaves, strangers, and, improbably, animals. The verse in Deuteronomy that elaborates on this aspect of the Sabbath repeats, twice, that slaves were not to work.[37]

Thus biblical Judaism did not obliterate the status demarcations between Israelite and resident stranger any more than it blurred the differences between men, women, slaves, and animals. What the Sabbath laws did, however, was to ameliorate those status differences by extending certain privileges, such as Sabbath rest, to all societal categories.

Christian theologian Harvey Cox emphasizes that Sabbath observance was the great precondition for acceptance into Jewish societies. In his recent analysis of "a Christian's journey through the Jewish year," Cox, a Harvard professor of divinity who is married to a Jewish woman, chose for his frontispiece two quotes. The first, from Isaiah, emphasizes that any would-be fellow traveler who did not carefully observe the Sabbath could not become part of God's covenantal community.[38] Within post-exilic Jewish society, Sabbath and kashruth observances emerged as two of the great shaping characteristics of Jewish communal life. Whatever their own beliefs and practices, students of Jewish history have been quite clear about the efficacy of quotidian Jewish behavior codes in preserving pre-emancipation Jewish societies despite often difficult circumstances. Cox's second quote is equally evocative. He chooses the famous words of the biblical Ruth, the archetypical sincere convert, who delineates her devotion to Jewish society, religion, and historical destiny. In fact, in ancient societies wives became part of their husbands' tribal culture. Cohen and other scholars demonstrate that non-

Jewish women who married into the Israelite or Judean communities became Jews, even when they lacked Ruth's Judaizing eloquence. They joined the ancient Jewish people during a time period before formal conversion procedures had been established, but they were expected to adopt the tribal religion of their husbands. As Cohen comments, "a wife's loyalty to her husband's religion would last as long as her loyalty to her husband."[39]

Processes for joining the Jewish people changed over time, and during the Hasmonean period the notion of formal conversion into Judaism emerged, at first exclusively for men, and was effected through ritual circumcision. Gradually, in "the late first or second century C.E. . . .the idea arose that gentile women (wives) too must convert; if they do not convert, they remain gentiles, even if married to a Jewish husband," because "a woman's personhood is beginning to emerge." At that time, "immersion became *a* conversion ritual for men and *the* conversion ritual for women." The status of mixed-married households and the details of the conversion process that we are familiar with through rabbinic Judaism began to be developed during the time of Ezra and Nehemiah and were "well under way by the time of the Maccabees, and . . . substantially complete by the time of the Talmud," largely in response to changes in the social structure of Jewish life:

> Neither Exodus nor Deuteronomy prohibits intermarriage with all non-Israelites, and both of them prohibit intermarriage with Canaanites only because it might lead to . . . idolatry. Biblical Israel was living on its own land and had no need for a general prohibition of intermarriage with all outsiders. Attitudes changed when conditions changed. In the wake of the destruction of the temple in 587 B.C.E., Judaea lost any semblance of political independence, the tribal structure of society was shattered, and the Israelites were scattered among the nations. In these new circumstances, marriage with outsiders came to be seen as a threat to Judaean (Jewish) identity and was widely condemned. The Judaeans sensed that their own survival depended on their ideological (or religious) and social separation from the outside world.[40]

The familiar principle of matrilineal descent became established after the Babylonian exile—as did most aspects of the rabbinic Judaism that has defined Jewish cultures for thousands of years. Advocates for patrilineality correctly assert that matrilineal kinship principles are not invoked in pre-exilic portions of the Hebrew Bible, and even in rabbinic law familial succession and status are mostly patrilineal within inmarried families. However, during the two millennia that shaped the Judaisms familiar today, the Jewish status of children followed the status of the Jewish mother. Non-Jews could join the Jewish community only by following the conversion prescriptions of rabbinic law.

For most of Diaspora Jewish history, entry of non-Jews into Jewish families and communities was discouraged not only by Jewish authorities but even more so by the non-Jews among whom they lived. Non-Jewish edicts against Christian or Moslem fraternizing or cohabiting with, or marrying into, local Jewish societies helped to shape Jewish antipathy toward proselytizing.[41] Tragic episodes resulted when Christian governments took unilateral revenge against Jewish communities that had accepted converts into Judaism. Despite the notable exceptions of a few philo-Judaic rulers and/or populations, the boundaries around Jewish societies were for the most part reinforced both by external and internal resistance to socializing and marriage across ethnoreligious lines.

In historical Jewish societies, social cohesiveness was not only structural but cultural as well. A densely interwoven fabric of distinctive Jewish religious behaviors, social norms, and linguistic, cultural, and structural characteristics made Jewishness a primary shaper of individual identity. Jewish identity was nurtured in communities in which Jews spoke Jewish languages, consumed distinctive food in ritualized milieus, prayed using ancient, religiously significant texts, and based much of their behavior on biblical and rabbinic literature and social prescriptions. Although Jews often borrowed much (and gave much to) the cultures around them, a richly particularistic Jewish flavor suffused their daily lives.

Physical and intellectual contact with non-Jewish neighbors was limited in most Jewish societies prior to emancipation. In historical Jewish communities, with notable exceptions in Spain and Italy, few Jews enjoyed systematic Western education before the seventeenth or eighteenth century. Lacking other outlets, the intellectual lives and perspectives of Jews were organized around sacred study and worship. These Jewish societies were profoundly albeit unevenly transformed during the eighteenth and nineteenth centuries, with advancing waves of social change leading to the emancipation of the Jews in France, Germany, and England, and considerably later in Eastern Europe. Gradually, the gates of Western educational and occupational opportunity opened to the Jews, providing access to modernity. Emancipators offered Jews the chance to emerge from their pariah status and, through education and the stripping away of many distinctive Judaic characteristics, to become part of humanity at large.

The insistence that Jews could only become part of civilized society by ceasing to be distinctively Jewish was in many ways a secularized legacy of the axiomatic Christian belief that Christianity had replaced Judaism, and that Christians displaced Jews as God's "chosen people." As some contemporary liberal Christian theologians analyze this brutal bargain, emancipation was colored by historical Christian thought:

> both anti-Judaism and displacement theology follow inevitably from the Christian claim that Jesus is the awaited Messiah, because this claim implies that Jews are blind to the real meaning of their own sacred texts. Since Christians have the "correct" interpretation, not only of the New Testament but of the Hebrew scriptures as well, Christians have obviously displaced the Jews in God's plan for the ages. The church has become, to use a theological term I find distasteful, the "new Israel."[42]

Although Jews were freed through emancipation from the physical walls of the ghetto and the experiential limitations of the shtetl, Christian distaste for Jews often survived secularization and the loss of faith. Jews and non-Jews alike perceived and talked about essential physical and psychological distinctions that demarcated Jews from their host societies but often disagreed as to whether these differences were congenital or societal in origin. Jewish distinctiveness was seen as a positive value, worthy of preservation, only by limited numbers of emancipated Jews.

Some Jews, especially in central and Western Europe, took the route of apostasy in their search for Western status. In these settings, outmarriage was an important strategy for reinforcing their acceptance into the middle and upper classes of Christian society. Thus, when we look at post-emancipation rates of "mixed marriage" in Western European communities, we are truly seeing the frequency of conversion into Christianity, rather than models of mixed marriage in contemporary American terms. A different pattern prevailed in Russia and Eastern Europe, where some of the brightest young Jews abandoned religion and worked to destroy racial and religious boundaries between peoples by devoting their energies to secular ideological social movements, including communism. Some atheistic Jews were primarily involved with other Jews who shared their worldview; others found non-Jewish mates in their social activism enterprises. Many Jews internalized negative images of Jewishness and saw the actual and potential erosion of ethnic boundaries as highly desirable.

For American Jews, the most striking diminishing of separation occurred after immigration. While early-twentieth-century America also had its share of antisemitism, as the decades passed, and Jews climbed up socioeconomic and educational ladders, the differences between Jews and their Christian neighbors paled. Nevertheless, social stratification remained in force and intermarriage rates were relatively low for decades. As Reform demographer Bruce Phillips notes,

> During the first half of the twentieth century, Jewish intermarriage was uncommonly low. Just after the turn of the century, Julius Drascher studied marriage records in New York City and found that the 1 percent rate of intermarriage among New York Jews was only slightly higher than the rate of interracial marriages among blacks. By mid-century, the statistics had not changed much. New Haven Jews studied in the late 1940s were the religious group least likely to be intermarried. Gerold Heiss similarly found that the intermarriage rate among Jews in midtown Manhattan (18.4 percent) was significantly lower than among both Protestants (33.9 percent) and Catholics (21.4 percent). In their classic work, *Beyond the Melting Pot,* Nathan Glazer and Daniel Moynihan described Jews as "the most endogamous of peoples."[43]

The idea of marrying out had important symbolic significance in American immigrant communities, despite the numerical infrequency of actual intermarriages. As we have seen, American literature, drama, and film portrayed the interethnic, interfaith romance as a paradigm for personal opportunities in the United States. Later, a sequence of historical events and trends, including the arrival of even "greener," non-Jewish, foreign-appearing immigrants, the acculturation and suburbanization of large portions of the Jewish community, World War II and its aftermath, the growth of the Equal Rights Movement and the celebration of ethnicity and multiculturalism in the late 1960s, and the impact of Israel in erasing images of Jews as weaklings and wanderers, played an important role in decreasing American perceptions of objectionable Jewish difference.

Paradoxically, as Jews became more and more accepted as white, middle-class Americans, their distinctive identity as Jews also became more and more acceptable. Jews in the United States, unlike Jews in France, Germany, and England, are not required to take on the protective coloration of secularization or non-differentiation as a ticket to acceptability. Jewishness is admired in many American societies. The permeable boundaries and multicultural ethos of contemporary American Jewish life, along with the widespread social acceptability of Jews as marital partners for non-Jews, have emerged gradually and are virtually unprecedented in Jewish history. Judaism as a faith tradition has been strikingly Americanized, creating commonalities and bridges between Jews and non-Jews who occupy the same socioeconomic, educational, geographical, and political milieus. As I have argued elsewhere, not only have American Jews created a coalesced American Judaism, they have also created a distinctly Jewish notion of what defines the "true" America, in their own image.[44]

In their deconstruction and reinterpretation of biblical texts and Jewish history, contemporary outreach activists are grounded in the values of coalesced American Judaisms. Rather than simply declaring the past irrelevant to present challenges, as some true secularists might do, they search to find precedents within the Jewish past. American Jews today often place a premium on integrative, rather than compartmentalized approaches. Thus, it becomes desirable to interpret passages that at one time were understood to emphasize and define the separations between Jews and pagan, or Christian, or Moslem societies, in contrast, as an illustration of permeable boundaries. In their depiction of some ancient Jewish societies as models of inclusiveness, these outreach activists have created a coalesced understanding of the Jewish past that is deeply appealing to American Jews precisely because it links their two worlds and makes them one.

Jews and Christianity Today

Within America's open society and its waning boundaries of ethnoreligious distinctiveness, large numbers of Jews have for decades been defined as much by what they were *not* as by what they were. As we have noted, Bellah wrote in 1987, "It is part of Jewish identity and the maintenance of the boundaries of the Jewish community to deny that Jesus is the Christ, the

Messiah,"[45] and Medding further suggested that "paradoxically, as the religious aspects of Judaism have become relatively less central to the core of Jewish identity, and shared feelings have become more important, being *not* Christian has taken on greater salience as a defining element of Jewishness."[46] Does not being a Christian still provide a rough basement for the lowest common denominator of Jewish identity? The answer, in the majority of mixed-married Jewish families, is emphatically "no."

The incorporation of Christian experiences is, of course, most pronounced within those households that are ideologically committed to raising their children "interfaith," that is, within two religious traditions. Thus, at a session entitled "Raising Children in Interfaith Households" held at the Dovetail Conference (Chicago, 2002), Jewish and Christian parents and their teenage children talked about the practical, day-to-day implications of their religious approaches. This session was attended by several young couples in the midst of raising or anticipating the raising of young children in two faiths. Jack Nagler, a Jewish father in his early forties, said that he and his wife took turns reading to their children before bedtime. The children were very fond of Bible stories. One night, Jack's daughter asked him to read the story of the crucifixion of Christ:

> It was my turn to read, and my daughter picked out the story of the crucifixion. I was stunned but realized I'd have to figure out how to handle it. I decided to read the story "straight"—that is, without all the little asides and comments I sometimes use when I'm not comfortable with the story I'm reading. So I read the story of the crucifixion straight, in a non-judgmental, not a sarcastic voice, and that really worked out well. My daughter enjoyed it, and I didn't feel freaked out. And I think it really showed our children that we are a unit, a family. That even though Mommy and I don't have the same religion, we support each other's religion. It's not just talk when we say we respect and support and share with each other, we really do.

It was very important to Jack Nagler to convey to his children that he and his wife comprised a parental unit that was not compromised by their differences of ethnic background or religious belief. He felt that by reading a classical Christian religious text to his daughter, he demonstrated in an unmistakable way that his respect and affection for his wife is in no way diminished by his being Jewish and her being Christian. As Nagler noted, the message his children will absorb is that interreligious cooperation is important. Loyalty to one particular religion is not a value they are being inculcated with in their home.

Families attending the Dovetail Conference seemed to be very intelligent and thoughtful, highly devoted both to the family and to the interfaith enterprise. They spent a great deal of time and energy on the religious education of their children, both through informal, home-based experiences and through attendance at church and synagogue supplementary schools. Some families chose to send their children only to church schools or only to synagogue schools, but they attended both types of worship services. Others had created specialized dual-religion communities, in some cases presided over by both a Christian clergyman and a rabbi.

Although the Dovetail adults emphasized over and over that their approach "was not syncretic," by which they explained emphatically that they "were not combining two religions and creating something new and different," their children did indeed emphasize the commonalities between Judaism and Christianity. As Kevin Nozick, the articulate fourteen-year-old son of a Catholic mother and a Jewish father, quipped, "Judaism and Christianity are really almost identical: they're only separated by about three laws—and one God!"

In many ways, the principled interfaith experience, as exemplified by the Dovetail group, illustrates the paradoxical American cultural bias toward the celebration of ethnoreligious differences as testimony to the sameness of all Americans. Americans share the experience of deriving from diverse, particularistic heritages, and the contemporary liberal ethos simultaneously accentuates and transcends differences. Valorizing the differences that unite, liberal Americans are fond of emphasizing commonalities that seem to span ethnic and religious boundaries.

Striking evidence of this ethos of unification through difference is found in department store decorations, magazine illustrations, and in a new species of greeting cards now proliferating in stationary shops, including those by the "Mixed Blessings Greeting Card Company." One card, for example, shows children who have respectively lit the solstice-based lights of Christmas, Hanukkah, and Kwaanza holding hands in front of their tribal candelabras. The message inside this card prays that the season of lights will "unite us all." These pictures, illustrations, decorations, and cards convey the impression that the messages of all religions are the same and it is only the packaging that differs.

Voices Along the Spectrum of Jewish-Christian Relations

However, perhaps surprisingly given the current cultural emphasis on unity, spokespersons for mixed-married enterprises at every level of inclusiveness or exclusivity were at great pains to distance themselves from the next most Christianizing group. Thus, parents who chose to raise their children within the socioreligious context of a Catholic-Jewish dialogue group, who chose to have their children participate in a "religious initiation ceremony" blending Catholic and Jewish elements at age thirteen, rather than an exclusively Jewish bar or bat mitzvah, spoke out vehemently about their differences from the "Jews for Jesus" or the "Messianic Jews" who are active in their geographic area:

> We are very different from Jews for Jesus or the Messianic Jews. They view Christianity as the logical fulfillment of Judaism—the completion of Judaism, as though Judaism were somehow limited or flawed. We don't believe that Judaism is lacking anything, and that Christianity is here to correct it. We want our children to understand and respect and feel attached to both religious traditions, to love them for what they are.

Just as the Dovetail Institute clearly differentiates itself from the approach of the "Jews for Jesus" or "Messianic Jews" movements, interfaith advocacy institutions and groups sometimes take pains to differentiate themselves from the Dovetail Institute. For example, Edmund Case declares that InterfaithFamily.com, which he publishes, "encourages interfaith families to participate in Jewish life and to raise their children as Jews." Case explains, "We distance ourselves from Dovetail and other organizations which encourage families to have two religions in the home."[47] In an op-ed piece for *The Jewish Week of New York,* Case clarifies that what he means by raising children as Jews "often includes participating in . . . Christmas and Easter celebrations." However, Case insists "that having a Christian holiday celebration in the home is the equivalent of affirming the divinity of Jesus" is "a notion that is simply ridiculous."[48]

Similarly, educators and leaders involved in communal outreach programs often try to distance themselves, specifically and by name, from the Dovetail approach. They emphasize that while their programs certainly teach respect for Christianity and the Christian partner, they do not teach Christianity per se as part of their curriculum. Their goal is to provide mixed-married couples, whether already married or contemplating marriage, with an appealing entry so that they will be attracted to the Jewish heritage and want to learn more.

Individual couples, also, are very interested in drawing distinctions between themselves and the next most Christianizing groups that they encounter. Families that describe themselves as "raising Jewish children" state emphatically that their primary family identification is "Jewish," even when their family activities include churchgoing at Christmas and Easter as well as home-based family observances. Similarly, those families who have the Christian holidays at home, but not at church, emphasize that differentiation.

Secular Jewish humanists also strongly distance themselves from the Jews for Jesus movement but welcome a mixture of celebrations and other behaviors if they are defined as "cultural" or "humanistic" rather than "religious." The Association of Humanistic Rabbis, for example, states, "We affirm the right of every Jew to marry whomever he/she chooses. We affirm the right of every rabbi to officiate at any marriage ceremony in which this free choice is exercised. We also affirm the right of every rabbi to co-officiate with any civil magistrate or minister of religion in such a ceremony as an act of respect for the dignity and culture of both the Jewish and non-Jewish partners."[49]

Secular Jewish humanists prefer the term "intercultural marriage" to "interfaith marriage," which they view as one narrow subset of intercultural marriage. As long as the two spouses do not believe in God or any kind of divine intervention and do not pray, "the conflict of competing religious beliefs is not an issue"[50] and humanistic Judaism "encourages both partners to share their cultures with each other and with their children."

> Humanistic Jews respect the cultural background of each partner, recognizing that there are important ethical values in all traditions. Thus, in an intermarried family, it is quite appropriate, if desired, to include a Christmas tree in the family's winter celebrations. In that case, both the hanukkia (the Hanukka candelabrum) and the tree serve to define and strengthen the family's twofold identity.[51]

At the exclusively Jewish end of the spectrum, those mixed-married families that hold the line and limit Christian observances to the homes of grandparents and other extended family members talk about their efforts, and what they perceive as their successes, with obvious pride. Their goal is to create a single-religion Jewish home, and to facilitate their children's identification with Judaism alone.

Mixed marriage is not necessarily just another name for assimilation. What is striking in the attitudes of mixed-married couples from the principled dual-faith end of the spectrum to the principled Jewish-only families is the strength of the resistance to simply going with the assimilatory slide and becoming part of the majority culture. On their own levels and in their own ways, many American mixed-married families want, in some fashion, to preserve some aspect of Jewish identity for themselves and their children.

Mixed-married religious commitments, however, usually do not comprise a sufficient impediment to assimilation to prevent its incremental pull. As Bruce Phillips points out, among adults who grew up in mixed-married families, only 8 percent describe themselves as Jewish by religion, 24 percent describe themselves as Christian, and 68 percent say they have no religion or are something else. In comparison, among adults who grew up in inmarried Jewish families, 92 percent describe themselves as Jewish by religion.[52] One of the reasons that mixed-married families tend not to transmit Jewish identity to their children is that so few of the households are exclusively Jewish in their religious cultural orientation. Just as children growing up in other mixed ethnoreligious American households come to accept as normative the blended traditions of their families, the American construct "Judeo-Christian tradition" is not an abstraction for many children of mixed marriage. While some of these children will eventually choose to become exclusively Jewish, the great majority of the children of mixed marriage bring their Judeo-Christian outlooks with them into their new homes and into their participation in American Jewish communal life.

Within the Conservative movement, the religious stakes move substantially closer to those of traditional Jewish societies. Only those children who have Jewish mothers, or who have been converted into Judaism through a Conservative or Orthodox rabbinic court, can remain within Conservative educational systems through bar/bat mitzvah in most synagogues and schools. Some Conservative schools do allow children with a Jewish father to enter and remain in school systems for some years in the hope that the entire family will move closer to Judaism and that conversion will result. This, of course, does not always happen. Several informants described what they defined as "heartbreaking" situations in which unconverted children of Jewish fathers and Christian mothers had been allowed to attend Conservative schools, only to be informed months before a bar/bat mitzvah ceremony that this life cycle event could not take place under Conservative auspices because the child in question was not halakhically Jewish.

Such stories, although they do not represent the official Conservative approach, nonetheless illustrate the erosion of boundaries between endogamous and exogamous family styles, even within the Conservative movement.

Within the multihued worlds of Orthodoxy, certain behavioral boundaries between Jewish and American behavior have been re-enforced over the past few decades. Overtly Christian observances are loudly discouraged and are in fact extremely unusual. Even American secularized cultural Christian activities such as Halloween costumes and candy collection, or Valentine's Day exchanges of cards and candies, have become increasingly rare in American Orthodox societies—although many Orthodox parents remember vividly that they were once not uncommon. Although certain cultural values and behaviors have most certainly been coalesced into Orthodox American personal and communal life, in other ways Orthodox Judaism has reinforced its boundaries, often erecting new barriers between Orthodoxy and other forms of Judaism. Orthodox schools, for example, often demand that students and their families comply with prescribed patterns of Orthodox behavior, thus drastically limiting the proportion of non-Orthodox families to those few who are willing to be Orthoprax (conforming to the practice of Orthodox Judaism if not to its belief system) for the duration of their children's schooling. Additionally, within Orthodox subgroups distinctions are drawn between one group and the next based on communal norms such as modesty of dress, rigor of avoiding contact with the opposite sex, and stringency of dietary law observance, among others.

Across the denominational spectrum, inmarried and conversionary Jewish parents often feel like they are fighting a war on two fronts against the infiltration of Christian observances into their children's lives. Parents in Atlanta, for example, described their ongoing vigilant battles with school officials to keep Christmas carols and plays and religious symbols such as creches out of their children's public school classrooms and assembly halls. Conservative and Reform endogamous couples who are synagogue members almost never incorporate Christmas trees or other religious-cultural symbols into their homes today (2 percent). Although Christmas trees in Jewish homes were not uncommon in the 1940s and 1950s, their use has diminished though the past few multicultural, pluralistic decades. Jewish-Jewish parents no longer feel they have to "make it up" to their children by incorporating aspects of Christmas observances into their Jewish households, so Christmas paraphernalia is found primarily in mixed-married households.

Such Conservative and Reform-affiliated parents work energetically to clarify the line between Jewish and Christian for their children. They have no objection to their children visiting Christian friends and seeing Christian observances in Christian homes. However, they want their children to understand that Judaism and Judaic practices are their heritage and do not require an admixture of Christianity to be festive and special. Many inmarried parents said they felt "undermined" when their children were invited to putatively Jewish homes of children they had met in religious schools, only to find Christmas trees and wreaths in what turned out to be mixed-married households. "How can I convince my children that Christmas and Easter don't belong in a Jewish home if their friends from Hebrew school are celebrating Christmas and Easter?" asked one mother.

The norms of the synagogue-member inmarried families in the Reform and Conservative movements have moved further away from religious syncretism. In contrast, mixed-married households have, as a group, accepted combining Judaism and Christianity as a communal norm. Although each mixed-married household may think of itself as individually and independently finding a way to "honor the faith tradition" of both parents, the social networks of mixed-married families, often heavily composed of other mixed-married families, reinforce the religious syncretism.

Conceptions of ethnicity, as we have noted, underwent profound change during the second half of the twentieth century. Constructionist theories of ethnicity view ethnic identity as fluid, continually being negotiated and renegotiated.[53] Some social scientists emphasize the importance of boundaries in creating discrete ethnic groups.[54] To use a homely metaphor, ethnographers who emphasize boundaries see ethnicity as a kind of shopping cart being pushed across time and space; the contents of the shopping cart keep changing, although the cart retains the same name, and thus its distinctiveness.[55] In contrast, another group of social scientists emphasizes "the nuclei, the centers of ethnic culture," rather than the boundaries, which may be porous and changing. According to them, it is exactly the "cultural stuff" at the heart of ethnic group life that maintains dynamic group distinctiveness and cohesiveness.[56]

In line with these social scientific theories, some policy planners take the approach that reinforcing the nucleus of Jewish life is the most effective strategy for transmitting commitments to the Jewish cultural heritage and the Jewish people to the next generation of Jews. Others insist that the community must reinforce its boundaries. The "nucleus" strategists believe that if they make Jewish experience and education compelling enough, they can de-emphasize boundaries. In the words of Barry Shrage, executive director of Boston's Combined Jewish Philanthropies, "if we show them how gorgeous Judaism is we can stop worrying so much about boundaries."[57]

Those who favor more well-maintained boundaries feel that the permeability of boundaries is in itself a betrayal of historical Jewish behaviors. A group of scholars and communal professionals who are concerned about maintaining boundaries has met over several years to consider policy statements that will express and publicize their concerns. Steven Bayme, director of research on contemporary Jewish life at the American Jewish Committee, is one of the most consistently outspoken of the anti-intermarriage activists. Bayme has repeatedly urged Jewish communal leaders to take a principled stand advocating endogamy and discouraging exogamy. He believes that the decline of personal and communal resistance to mixed marriage is in part responsible for its dramatic growth and acceptability in the Jewish community.[58]

Similarly, Jack Wertheimer, provost and professor of American Jewish history at the Conservative Jewish Theological Seminary, and the late Charles Liebman, emeritus Bar Ilan professor of sociology and former director of the Argov Center, frequently warn American Jews not to "surrender" to intermarriage. Wertheimer and Liebman see the current decline of Jewish communal resistance to mixed marriage as nothing less than a failure of loyalty to Jewish history and a lack of will to survive as a culture and as a people. As Wertheimer summarizes:

> for any community determined to ensure the survival of its own island in the pluralist sea, the very minimum required is that it be willing to assert without apology the absolute worth of its traditions and beliefs. For the leaders of American Jewry, meeting this requirement would mean adopting an altogether

new tack. It would mean speaking forthrightly and directly about where, and how, and why Judaism dissents from the universalistic ethos of the culture at large. And it would especially mean speaking on behalf of those distinctive commandments, beliefs, and values for the sake of which Jews over the millenia—born Jews and those who have joined themselves to the Jewish people through conversion alike—have willingly, and gratefully, set themselves apart.[59]

These sentiments have been actively opposed by a broad spectrum of outreach activists. JOI's Rabbi Olitzky dismisses the concerns of "inreach" advocates as a mere "euphemism for exclusion." He describes inreach leaders as a kind of elitist cabal and reduces their plea for support and advocacy for inmarried families as a call "for the return of the stigma against intermarriage."[60] Countering him, inreach activists like Bayme, Liebman, and Wertheimer argue that the increasing prominence and acceptability of mixed-married households, and the culturally reinforced religious syncretism within those households have led to a widespread change in cultural norms. They are afraid that the American Jewish community has crossed a threshold in which unambiguous Jewishness is no longer a societal value. Echoing the arguments of Wertheimer, et al., Jewish parents who want passionately for their children to establish Jewish—not Judeo-Christian—homes often say that they feel lonely and abandoned when Jewish public policy planners seem indifferent to their battle for religious authenticity. They say they do not particularly wish for a "return of the stigma against intermarriage," to use JOI's terminology. However, they do long for clarity in the Jewish communal approach to religion in the home.

Statements from both sides of this issue show how individual behaviors are embedded in the social networks that provide the contexts for people's lives. Personal behavior is profoundly influenced by a perception of what other people are doing, as Malcom Gladwell has convincingly argued to a broad audience. Certain behaviors can be considered transgressive or unacceptable for a very long period of time. However, once enough individuals in a particular social network perceive these behaviors to be widespread or popular, a "threshold" has been passed and societal expectations go over a "tipping point." From that time forward, the once-transgressive behavior is viewed as normative, and persons will be pulled toward it, all other things being equal. Indeed, once the threshold has been passed, previously normative values are often viewed as socially undesirable.[61] (One example of this phenomenon is the feeling that some stay-at-home mothers had in the 1980s that they were transgressing societal expectations that they be labor force participants; in contrast, working mothers in the 1950s were widely regarded as transgressing social norms. The "tipping point" for this social transformation occurred during the 1970s.)

American Jewish attitudes toward intermarriage provide a fascinating example of this type of societal transvaluation. Exogamy was long considered transgressive behavior, and those who advocated on behalf of endogamy had societal approval. The figure from the 1990 National Jewish Population Study that galvanized the American Jewish community, indicating that among the most recent marriages 52 percent were mixed marriages, was important (regardless of its reliability) because it suggested that a behavioral threshold had been reached. This apparent behavioral "tipping" facilitated the "tipping" phenomenon in Jewish societal norms. Today, as recent research shows, exogamy is an accepted fact of life, and those who advocate on behalf of endogamy are often derided as reactionary or even racist. In sociological terms, advocates for endogamy have become the new transgressors.

Recent research shows that these changed communal norms have practical effects. Their impact extends to congregational life. Rabbis and congregational leaders often are reluctant to "push" Jewishness and do not expect non-Jewish spouses to engage in any meaningful way with Judaism. They focus on making non-Jews feel welcome rather than mentoring them toward joining the Jewish community. The recent systematic study of congregational responses to interfaith issues by the Cohen Center for Modern Jewish Studies at Brandeis found that many congregations "succeed at helping interfaith families to feel welcome" but "do less well at encouraging them to progress on their Jewish journey." Although mixed-married couples experienced these congregations as "warm and gracious," they were puzzled at the lack of encouragement toward achieving "greater ritual and spiritual engagement." Along with changed communal norms, low Jewish expectations seem also to stem from insecurity about the ultimate attractiveness of Jewish activities: "I guess we could do more, but I'm not sure what we could do, since we don't want to turn people off."[62]

The same study found that conversion is not really supported within many congregations. Researchers found that most "senior rabbis did not, as a rule, actively invite non-Jewish members to consider conversion." Thus, although "the rabbi is in a unique position to open a dialogue about conversion," such

conversations seldom happened, "even when the rabbi suspected that a member might be considering conversion or when they had observed their growing engagement with Judaism."[63]

Finally, the Brandeis study found that even when non-Jews have converted to Judaism, most "synagogues do not provide mentoring after conversion." Preoccupied with welcoming in non-Jewish spouses and trying to determine whether or not it is advisable or necessary to "draw boundaries regarding their participation in ritual and governance," little thought is addressed to the very substantial Jewish support needs of conversionary households. One example of this attention toward mixed-married rather than conversionary households concerned holiday celebrations. Researchers were told that "converts still have to deal with non-Jewish family members around Christian holidays, but outreach programs such as the "December Dilemma" are targeted toward interfaith families. Synagogues seem to take the approach that once conversion is completed, problems cease, and this is far from the reality."[64]

One rabbi, referring disparagingly to the common practice of not giving converts follow-up support while continuing to labor mightily to attract and please non-Jewish spouses, joked grimly, "Yes, they complain—and rightly— that we leave them dripping at the mikvah." He and other Reform rabbis who try to maintain advocacy for unambiguously Jewish families, whether they are born-Jewish or conversionary-Jewish households, often feel that they are also being undermined by widespread communal attitudes that it is no longer strategic—and maybe not even moral—to privilege families who are Jewishly committed.

It should be noted that certain types of programs may provide mentoring both to mixed-married and to converted populations without being specifically geared toward this goal. For example, the birthright israel program brings college students to Israel for a short but intensive experience. Because the program focuses on students who have never been to Israel on a previous educational trip, many young people who grew up in mixed-married or conversionary families participate in birthright israel trips. Many find that the trip gives them the opportunity to explore their Jewish connections in a very non-intimidating setting.

American Jews (with the exception of limited groups of neoconservatives and some Orthodox Jews) share deeply liberal intellectual and psychological mindsets with other well-educated white Americans.[65] Most Jews like to believe that many conflicts can be solved through compromise and negotiation, and that situations can be seen in a variety of ways. Younger and better-educated Jews often display an almost visceral repulsion to the idea of singling out any one group, including one's own descent group, for particularly favorable treatment. Chauvinism of all kinds invites disapproval or open scorn on college campuses and in many intellectual circles, and it is no longer socially acceptable to articulate manifestations of religious prejudice, racism, jingoism, mysogyny, homophobia, or even "speciesism," the preferential treatment of the human species.

Accordingly, American Jews pride themselves on their empathy for, and feelings of solidarity with, all people of good will. Jewish insistence on inclusiveness is partially a reaction to the fact that Jews historically have been frequently vilified as "exclusive" or "clannish." Jews individually and as a group have often endured educational, occupational, and social exclusion, not only in Europe but in the United States until relatively recently as well. As a result, the historical Jewish concept of a "chosen people" articulated in tribal passages in the Hebrew Bible or the Jewish liturgy make many American Jews uneasy. Most find unappealing and/or embarrassing the extensive classical rabbinic texts that seem designed to separate Jews from non-Jews and to maintain coherent boundaries. Although some still sense that there is an essential core of Jewishness that makes Jews more comfortable with each other than with non-Jews, this attitude is far more prevalent among older American Jews than among their children and grandchildren.

This avoidance of the appearance of chauvinism, not surprisingly, has had an enormous general impact on the way younger American Jews interface with their own Jewishness. On one hand, many look down on the old habit of Jewish newspaper reading in which every article—especially those involving scandal or tragedy—is anxiously perused to be sure that no Jew has been exposed as dishonest or died in an accident. The colloquial term "M.O.T.," Member Of the Tribe, much in use by the first suburbanizing Jews in the 1940s and 1950s as they surreptitiously looked for other Jews who might be living in their previously *Judenrhein* neighborhoods, has virtually disappeared from the vocabulary of younger American Jews.

On the other hand, many young American Jews are fascinated by their Jewish heritage, although they are not quite sure what Jewishness is, or what it might mean to them. This fascination with Jewishness surfaces in cultural phenomena such as the great popularity of Adam Sandler's "Hanukkah

Song," played repeatedly by deejays across the country and on cable concert specials, which provided listeners with lists of celebrities who are putatively half-Jewish and even "one-quarter-Jewish."

The American Jewish preference for inclusiveness also helps to explain the changed norms in personal and communal responses to rising rates of mixed marriage, since inclusiveness feels more "comfortable" to most American Jews than exclusiveness does. Unprecedentedly high rates of mixed marriage are experienced in the context of the delight and pride American Jews feel about their perceptions that Jewish tradition harmonizes with American ideals, partially because these feelings resonate with the powerful appeal of the "inclusivity and outreach" message.

10

SPECULATING ON JEWISH FUTURES

Is Advocating for Jewish Families Racism?

The erosion (but not disappearance) of tribal loyalties in the Jewish community is symptomatic of attitudes in the larger liberal American community as well. Jewish squeamishness about chauvinism is part of the general liberal American emphasis on the individual and the individual's interpretation, with an accompanying reluctance to ascribe privileged status to any one group or stance. In some cases, nonjudgementalism veers into relativism. The American intellectual attempt to understand all points of view and to assign them equal value has been strikingly evident in some academic responses to the events of September 11, 2001. Chester Finn, for example, reports that many educators are made profoundly uncomfortable by the use of the word "patriotism." Finn argues that "assumptions forged during the Vietnam conflict and then tempered by the post-modern doctrines of multiculturalism and diversity have overwhelmingly shaped the pedagogical and curricular guidelines for elementary and secondary school teachers."[66] Highly educated liberal Americans often have trouble articulating an absolute loyalty to their own country, even after the bloody World Trade Center and Pentagon attacks.

It should not be surprising, then, that within this liberal ethos the attempt of a particular ethnoreligious group to promote endogamy and to advocate against exogamy can appear to be a racist enterprise. In an October 14, 2001

New York Times Magazine column, for example, Randy Cohen "The Ethicist," was asked the following question: "Some friends and I use a Jewish Internet dating service. When I mentioned an ad placed by a Hispanic woman who likes to date Jewish men, a female friend of mine remarked that 'they should stay away from our stuff.' I argued that the Hispanic woman was upfront about her ancestry and so did nothing wrong. Please shed some light.[67]

Cohen transmits a very interesting gender difference in his response to this question. The male questioner assumes that any honest American has the right to use the Jewish internet dating service. However, the female friend is upset with the idea that those eligible Jewish men who use the dating service looking for Jewish women—a category of persons reputedly in short supply—may be captured by an enterprising non-Jewish woman. The first paragraph of Cohen's answer reflects the current assumptions of the great majority of American Jews that intermarriage is inevitable, and not necessarily problematic, in an open society:

> You can, of course, be Hispanic and Jewish—Jews in Barcelona do it every day—and if that's the case here, problem solved. But even if the controversial Hispanic woman is a gentile, I still see no problem. She has been open about her background and her desires. (Although she may want to examine the feelings that draw her to a group rather than a particular individual.) If another participant in the dating service finds her appealing, then the two of them can rendezvous. It's not for some third party to veto that decision. The Jewish dating service should be a way for people who wish to date Jews—perhaps primarily but not exclusively other Jews—to do so; it ought not be a segregated Semite preserve.

The second paragraph of Randy Cohen's answer effectively articulates the reasons why many American Jews are concerned about the impact of mixed marriage on Jewish families and communities:

> Needless to say, a whites-only dating service would be repugnant, trading on racism, on superficial characteristics over which people have no control. By contrast, a Jewish dating service defines people by their behavior and beliefs, by something volitional. In theory, anyone can choose to embrace Jewish customs and to search for a like-minded spouse with whom to establish a Jewish household and live according to Jewish precepts. That is, members of a minority culture, eager to preserve and practice a way of life, may honorably seek

each other out online or in person. That isn't to say, however, that you may impose this belief on other people. So let the Hispanic woman and her Jewish suitors dance the night away.

Note that Cohen begins this paragraph by making sure that readers understand he is not a racist. He distances Jewish concern about endogamy from racism. The concept of Jewish peoplehood is fraught with discomfort for most American Jews today, especially outside of the Orthodox world. As we have noted, the traditional Jewish construct of the "chosen people," repeatedly articulated in biblical texts and foundational to Jewish thinking for much of Jewish history, has been rejected or explained out of recognition by many American Jewish thinkers, as well as ordinary American Jews.

What is less often recognized, however, is that the cultural coherence of Jewish ethnoreligious identity construction is blurred by the enormous popularity of certain aspects of Jewish culture in the external American culture. Coalescence implies not only the absorption of American values and behaviors into Jewish culture but also the incorporation of Jewish cultural markers into American culture—the Americanization of Judaism and the Judaization of America.

The Jewish tendency to ceremonialize and ritualize, for example, has been incorporated into the lives of sophisticated, well-educated non-Jewish as well as Jewish young Americans, especially in major metropolitan areas with large Jewish populations. The process through which this has happened is described in social network theory as "brokering": an elite group within a particular cultural stratum introduces values and behaviors to others in the cohort and helps to normalize them. For example, Jewish prominence in the entertainment industries has led to Jews brokering many Jewish words, phrases, and attitudes into television, film, and media communications, and from there into general American culture. (College students have trouble believing that words like "chutzpah" and "schlep" were once not part of the standard American vocabulary.) As another example, a front-page article in the *Forward* describes a new trend among Christian couples to incorporate Jewish wedding customs such as breaking the glass and shouting "mazel tov" after the ceremony has been completed.[68] Similarly, in the incident described below, the prominence of Jews in many young adult friendship networks of highly educated, high-status occupational cohorts serves as an institutional conduit transporting Jewish ceremonial behaviors.[69]

According to recent reports, some unmarried New Yorkers who are not content to simply live together without benefit of marriage want their co-habitation to be recognized by their social network. One couple created a ceremony called a "Commitzvah," described in a recent book, *Unmarried to Each Other: The Essential Guide to Living Together as An Unmarried Couple.* Rebecca Meade writes about the ceremony created by Joe Lowndes and Priscilla Yamin, "who are both finishing their Ph.D.s in political science at the New School":

> Lowndes said he had always wanted to be unmarried—"I was an activist and anarchist for years, and am not comfortable with my private relationships being wrapped up with state policies," he explained—but it was not until he met Yamin that he knew he had found the woman he wanted to be unmarried to. After seven years together, they held what they called a "Commitzvah," at which they exchanged vows, drank from a kiddush cup, and handed out little bells that friends and family were asked to ring at the moment the unmarriage was sealed. The Commitzvah is described in a chapter of the book about com-mitment ceremonies. . . . Yamin said that being formally unmarried did add an unexpected emotional dimension to the relationship, and that both families en-joyed the Commitzvah.[70]

These cultural borrowings take place in an environment in which marry-ing a Jew has a certain cache among segments of the Christian community. Thus, Ellen O'Brien writes about her mother, who "has Scottish ancestors, was raised Episcopalian, and later took her own children to a Unitarian church," and who is now relentlessly pressuring her daughter to meet and marry a Jewish man. O'Brien's mother "saw a menorah that would make a great Christmas gift for me" and "offered to buy me an introductory subscrip-tion to JDate.com, the Internet dating service, for (mostly) Jewish singles." To further her goals, O'Brien's mother has begun acting like a Jewish mother herself, or at least like "some moms portrayed on silly sitcoms," going so far as to take a summer vacation at a Jewish retreat center, "Camp Isabella Freedman," where she "heard lectures on things such as the Jewish literary tradition, the Jewish-American experience, great persons in Jewish history, and the legacy of Jewish humor."[71]

Jewish cultural and intellectual prominence, socioeconomic successes and acculturation, and current social acceptability have led to a situation in which Jewishness is viewed by many as a particularly appealing version of

American identity. When Chinese American author Gish Jen wants to describe a "typical American," she makes her teenage Chinese American heroine model herself on Jewish girls in Scarsdale.[72] Philip Roth picks up on this unprecedented normalization of Jewishness by having his African American protagonist in *The Human Stain* pass for being white by passing for being Jewish.[73]

Although American culture seems to celebrate ethnic distinctiveness, it undermines ethnic exclusivity, as illustrated by the question posed to "The Ethicist." Whether a person comes by their ethnicity through family inheritance or through choice (i.e., conversion), they are encouraged to blend one or more ethnoreligious traditions. Thus, syncretic trends within American Jewish societies reflect and have been reinforced by the open celebration of religious syncretism in American popular culture. In television programs such as *Inlaws, Northern Exposure, Thirtysomething, Mad About You,* and *L.A. Law,* among others, as well as in programs produced for children such as the previously discussed *As Told By Ginger,* American mainstream television indoctrinates viewers to believe that religious syncretism is fair, highly evolved, and truly American. In these programs religious syncretism is not just tolerated—it is a desideratum. The practical syncretism of interfaith households and their social networks is thus reinforced by the cultural milieu, through such vehicles as television programs, and also by the popular cultural merging of diverse religious faiths.

Faith in the Family

Parents are not always aware of the extent to which their own behavior influences their children, not only as they are growing up but when they become adults as well. Sociologist of religion Robert Wuthnow notes that the greatest influence occurs when children see "their parents engaged in these activities rather then doing them only for the sake of the children." He adds that although most Americans "claim to have developed a more private, individualistic or idiosyncratic view of spirituality as adults," there is an important link "between this view of spirituality and how they come to understand prayer from their parents."[74]

As long as a household psychologically retains a connection with two faiths, our interview research showed, many mixed-married spouses feel emotionally divided, even unfaithful, as if their Jewish loyalties are at war with their empathetic family feelings. If they "deprived" their Christian spouse of Christian symbols, many felt guilty. On the other hand, if they re-incorporated Christian symbols they had been determined not to incorporate, many also felt guilty about that.

Powerful moments such as the birth of a child, the death of a parent, a shake-up in the workplace, or the divorce of a friend often precipitate spiritual responses and re-evaluations of decisions on the religious character of the home. In some cases, these lead to a deepening attachment to Judaism and to the Jewish community. In other cases, the resoluteness of early decisions as to the Jewish character of the household gives way to a variety of new negotiations. For mixed-married couples who have decided to raise children as Jews only, it is difficult to maintain an exclusively Jewish household environment.

These widespread Christian aspects of mixed-married family life stand in contrast to families in which the born-Christian partner has become a Jew by choice. In conversionary households, Jews by choice usually feel that they and their households are unambivalently Jewish. Jews by choice often announce to their own Christian parents and siblings, "We are a family. Please don't send our children Christmas presents or Easter baskets." In mixed-married households that have pledged to raise their children as Jews, however, it is much more difficult for parents to maintain an unambivalently Jewish profile. As long as one spouse does not consider him- or herself to be a Jew, it is hard to exclude Christian rituals, ceremonies, and culture from family life.

Many non-Jewish spouses cheerfully participate in their Jewish children's holiday celebrations. Nevertheless, some of them find themselves feeling increasingly resentful about the fact that their children are growing up in a faith tradition different from theirs. Even when they say they have been warmly received by family members and Jewish synagogue communities, non-Jewish spouses often find themselves longing for their own traditions in their own households. Some report that they are disturbed by their children's use of Hebrew in household and holiday prayers—and yet they have decided that they do not wish to learn Hebrew themselves. As we have seen, some say they harbor deep distaste for organized religion and look forward to the day their children are old enough to share these feelings.

Parents who intend to raise children "as Jews" often do not realize the extent to which extended family members can influence the religious identity of their children, especially as they grow into adolescence and beyond and may be looking for alternative paths as they rebel against parental role models. Wuthnow argues that "the role of grandparents has been virtually ignored in recent theories of religious development," despite the fact that "there is often a direct influence" exerted by grandparents and other family members.[75] My study shows that adolescent children grow close to extended family members on the basis of many factors, including their own personalities and intellectual and extracurricular interests. Non-Jewish grandparents, aunts, uncles, and cousins often become admired role models for many raised-Jewish children in mixed-married households. Extended family members are often accessed due to their status in the "kinship" system: although their relationship with—and ultimate influence on—children of mixed-married families varies, and is unpredictable, when the family has not made an unambiguous commitment to Judaism children often view the faith traditions that even loosely related family members embody as a legitimate part of their heritage.

Challenges to the Transmission of Jewish Culture

Distinctiveness is a necessary attribute for the ethnoreligious survival of minorities, history suggests. The fate of minority groups living in open societies has often concluded in disappearance over time, largely through mixed marriage and religious/cultural intermixing.[76] Moreover, today the cultural context surrounding mixed marriages advocates on behalf of doubleness by normalizing religious syncretism and delegitimating the idea of Jewish religious exclusivity. Together the current combination of (1) overall American Jewish coalescence, (2) high rates of mixed marriage, and (3) religious syncretism in mixed-married households may construct powerful barriers to cultural transmission. This combination of factors crosses a threshold where the balance of Jewishness versus non-Jewishness (primarily Christianity in the United States) tips toward Christianity. Jewish societies in the past absorbed many aspects of other cultures, but historically these borrowings were adapted to rabbinic mandates. Cultural borrowings were incorporated into Jewish societies that spoke Jewish languages (Yiddish, Ladino, and Judeo-Arabic), lived according to a dense network of Jewish mores and customs and religious strictures, and were often significantly separated from the societies around them. Comparing the contemporary situation to one oft-cited historical period, Maimonides imported Aristotelian philosophy, and medieval Spanish exegetes sometimes wrote erotic secular poetry, for example, but they were deeply steeped in the intricacies of rabbinically prescribed lifestyles and intellectual preoccupations.

Jewish borrowings in the past took cultural materials and made them Jewish. Second, and equally critical, the cultural borrowings of Jewish societies in the past were, almost without exception, not religious in nature. Bringing melodies similar to medieval church music into a synagogue, for example, does not have the same impact as bringing the ideas, beliefs, and behaviors of the Christian church into Jewish households. Adapting Russian blini and borscht to the Jewish cuisine is not the same thing as taking Jewish children to church to celebrate holidays.

Expanding the Jewish Renaissance

Inmarriage and mixed marriage occur according to clear patterns. Inmarriage—and strong Jewish connections in mixed-married families—are closely correlated to three factors: (1) Jewish education, both formal and informal, that is intensive and continues through the teen years; (2) a Jewishly connected home that provides multifaceted Jewish experiences in family settings; and (3) Jewish friendship circles. Each of these alone, and exponentially all three of these together, dramatically predisposes an individual to marry a Jew and to establish a new Jewish family. In other words, the more Jewishly connected the parental family and the more Jewish education an individual receives, the more likely it is that the individual will establish a Jewishly connected home of his or her own.

Segments of the American Jewish community are experiencing a cultural renaissance that, interestingly enough, is occurring simultaneously with the challenges of syncretism in other parts of the community. For mixed-married families as well as inmarried families, the combination of Jewishly active family life and rich formal and informal educational experiences is demonstrably the most effective way to generate interest in Jewish connections among children. In Bruce Phillips's study of the children of intermarriage, he found that the three factors that contributed to return inmarriage—that is, a child of intermarriage marrying a Jew—were (1) having a non-Jewish parent who identifies as secular rather than Christian, (2) consciously being raised as a Jew, and (3) receiving some type of formal Jewish education. Of his adult children of intermarriage respondents with all three factors, 30 percent married Jews. Phillips points out that among adult children of inmarriage the same combination of factors— that is, a combination of family Jewish connections and formal Jewish education—yields more than double the inmarriage rate. However, among adult children of mixed marriage missing even one of these factors, only a tiny proportion married Jews.[77]

Thus, many studies indicate that for both inmarried and mixed-married families, the most effective strategy for cultural transmission is for the Jewish community to enrich Judaic experiences and knowledge across age, denominational, and geographic lines. Alan Dershowitz argues that "for Judaism to become a transmittable civilization in an integrated world where Jews do not experience isolation, discrimination, and victimization, Jewish learning must become *accessible* to integrated and secular Jews. It must become *usable* to them in their daily lives, much the way it was usable in a different way to their ancestors." American Jews must reverse their "collective drift toward Jewish illiteracy" by shifting "resources toward Jewish education," if they are to kindle a passion for Jewish connections within American Jews of all ages.[78]

Jewish experiences, including formal and informal educational encounters, facilitate the process of "anamnesis, an antidote to amnesia, or forgetting."[79] Research shows that religious and cultural renaissance-building serves multiple purposes. First, it increases personal and familial Jewish connections and social networks; second, it maximizes the likelihood that single Jews will be imbued with a desire to create their own Jewish families; and finally—and very germane to this discussion—it enhances the dynamism and vibrancy of the Jewish experience into which outreach efforts bring the non-Jewish spouses of Jews.

This two-pronged approach of advocating for Jewish religious unambiguousness and nurturing wider Jewish cultural renaissance comprises a challenging assignment. Nevertheless, cultural resistance has its own sociological caché. As Wuthnow, Iannaccoce, and others have shown, bland, generic, mainstream Christian denominations have inexorably lost ground, while those Christian denominations that make demands on their adherents and are characterized by dissonance with the general culture have grown dramatically stronger.[80] Evidence suggests that, rather than fleeing from difference and commitment, some groups of Americans are searching for spirituality and community, and they often turn to countercultural, clearly defined religious societies to find these things. Dissonance with American culture—and even difficulty—may be assets for minority cultures.

Moreover, Richard Alba and others have shown that it is precisely the most well-educated and socioeconomically successful ethnic Americans who strive hardest to transmit distinctive ethnoreligious traditions to their children.[81] American Jews—including most mixed-married Jews—overwhelmingly fall into this demographic cohort. Brandeis's Cohen Center for Modern Jewish Studies evaluation of Reform outreach programs demonstrates that mixed-married couples greatly prefer substantive, mainstream educational programs rather than less rigorous programs "primarily focused on issues of acceptance and religious diversity," which are specifically aimed at interfaith families.[82]

Ultimately, American Jewish communities will create their own list of priorities, either through a process of thoughtful deliberation or through default and indecision. The inclusive model is currently attractive because of its "political correctness," since it avoids boundary maintenance and judgementalism—except against those who themselves seem to be passing judgement. The alternate communal strategy for dealing with the challenges of rising rates of mixed marriage calls for focusing communal will on the intensification of a broad spectrum of identifiably Jewish cognitive and experiential opportunities for Jews of all ages. This strategy is opposed by some because it calls for the painful reallocation of communal resources and difficult assessments as to what comprises authentic Jewish activities and attitudes. Moreover, such an emphasis would almost inevitably be accompanied by some shrinkage in terms of computable Jewish population size. Serious economic and political ramifications accompany a reduction in the number of persons who can be counted as Jews, and some observers are frightened at the prospect of a smaller Jewish community.

Jewish communal laypeople and leaders alike are concerned about the occurrence and ramifications of mixed marriage in their own families. Their concern is not based on "racism," as is sometimes alleged, but on familial and communal issues of continuity, popularly articulated in the question, "Will my grandchildren be Jewish?" As we have seen, by seeking to transmit what *New York Times* ethicist Randy Cohen calls their "minority culture" and their Jewish "way of life" on to the next generation, American Jews today are responding not only to the models of Jewish history but also to the models provided by their non-Jewish ethnic neighbors. The contemporary American Jewish quest for cultural continuity is, to an extent not often realized, an articulation not only of traditional, historical Jewish values but of prevalent American values as well.

Intermarried Christian theologian Harvey Cox argues Christian spouses of Jews have a responsibility to respect "the particularity of Judaism and its continued place in God's economy" and to take "every measure possible to ensure that Jews—as a people—will continue to be numbered among the peoples of the earth." According to Cox, this conviction must start with an unshakable commitment to "one of the most basic of all Jewish beliefs—that the child of a Jewish mother is a child of the covenant, a Jew, and should be recognized as such":

> The bottom line is the question, "What about the children?" In short, many Jews fear that since they constitute a minority in most places in the world, every mixed marriage puts the next generation's Jewishness at risk. These fears are hardly groundless. Statistics show that the children of mixed marriages are far less likely to think of themselves as Jewish than are children of marriages between two Jews. The grandchildren of mixed marriages are even less likely to do so. Christians need to understand why Jews view this prospect with such dread. At some level, most Jews feel very intensely that something of immeasurable importance would be lost, not just to them, but to everyone, if all Jews were to disappear from the earth. I agree . . . a stark demographic reality looms into view. There are only about fourteen million Jews on earth. . . . In contrast, there are an estimated two billion Christians in the world, and the number continues to grow. . . . We need to reassure Jews by words and actions that we are also committed to a future for the Jewish people.[83]

Peoplehood and the American Jews

Discussions about the character of mixed-married households are complicated by vagueness about racial, ethnic, and religious definitions in America today. Blurred boundaries, of course, are not limited to segments of the Jewish community. Even United States Census planners have found it necessary to acknowledge the widespread blending of ethnic and racial heritages in the lives of increasing numbers of Americans by creating new subcategories.[84]

Jonathan Sarna notes that "mixed marriages of every kind" have "proliferated in the United States, crossing ethnic, religious, and racial lines":

> Swedish, Norwegian, German, Italian, and Irish Americans all, according to 1980 census data, experienced intermarriage rates in excess of 60 percent. Among Catholics, intermarriage rates among young people exceeded 50 percent. . . . In the much smaller Greek Orthodox Church, by the early 1990s fully two-thirds of all marriages involved a partner who was not Greek Orthodox. . . . Asian Americans and African Americans likewise witnessed dramatic upswings in intermarriage.[85]

Jewishness has historically been more complex than either religion, culture, or ethnicity alone. This sometimes makes Jewish connections seem difficult to understand or even offputting to Christian spouses "because Christianity requires *seeking* the covenant—getting baptized, going to church for the sacraments—the idea of being born into a faith is unfamiliar . . . many Gentiles are unaware that Jews see themselves as a people, a nation, a tribe, and not just a religion."[86] Rather than being defined as the faith of an individual soul, Jewishness more closely matches one commonly recognized definition of an ethnic group, as "a collectivity within a larger society having real or putative common ancestry, memories of a shared historical past, and a cultural focus on one or more symbolic elements defined as the epitome of their peoplehood."[87] For Jews, all of these components of peoplehood, ethnicity, culture, and religion were combined during the two-thousand-year postexilic period and have continued to be a compelling construct.

Current assessments of the challenge of mixed marriage are linked to concepts of Jewish peoplehood. As Michael Walzer notes while discussing the work of Israeli philosopher and social critic Avishai Margalit, "the common life of people who share ethnicity, history, culture, or religion, and who have a sense of one another as fellow members" today is often described by the term "thick human relations." Boundaries are necessary in order to define the groups to whom we have special responsibilities, note Walzer and Margalit. The most powerful example of this type of thick relationship is, of course, the family unit.[88]

Remembered, shared experiences, along with ethnicity and religion and culture, were interwoven in ideas of Jewish peoplehood for millennia. Partially because of their small numbers and often vulnerable position, and partially out of loyalty to their rich cultural and religious heritage, and partially through their daily obligations, Jews felt themselves to be linked in a thick relationship, part of a people that shared some characteristics of family. Jewish peoplehood was not a race, however, since persons not born into this relationship could join through conversion and become part of the people by linking their destiny to that of the Jewish community.

Despite recent sociological focus on personalism and the individual, it was by formally joining Jewish social networks that fellow travelers became bona fide Jews. Jewish social networks were strengthened by religious traditions, an emphasis on widespread text-based religious education, and religiously mandated communal responsibilities toward vulnerable populations, including the bereaved and deceased. Jewish holidays and texts reinforced communal identification with the saga of an ancient, shared narrative that shaped and defined the people. And almost always, Jewish relatedness was cemented by the boundaries imposed by antisemitism and internal and external xenophobia.

Retaining a sense of Jewish peoplehood is particularly complex in the United States. The American homeland arouses in most Jews a deep sense of allegiance, affection, loyalty, and responsibility. Life in America—with all its freedom and openness—is also pleasurable. The freedom to choose one's spouse is profoundly emblematic of both America's freedoms and its pleasures. Celebrating at his son's wedding to a Vietnamese young woman "who as a baby escaped with her family from Saigon as it was falling," a Jewish doctor "observing the multicultural mélange" commented happily, "This is what life is all about in America, what makes the train ride all the more fun."[89]

At the same time, even in America Jews across the spectrum have a lingering sense that their destiny is linked, perhaps in unforeseen ways, to the destiny of Jewish people around the world. At a panel discussion in the closing session of the Dovetail Conference in Chicago (2002) Jews and their non-Jewish spouses poured out their hearts about their differences regarding Israel. "I can't help it, I feel safe," said one woman. "I was raised as a Protestant, and I don't feel in danger. It's hard for me to relate to why it is that David feels so vulnerable." Her husband also struggled for words to express himself: "We need Israel. The Jewish people need Israel. There has to be place for us, that really is ours, where we don't have to be dependent upon the kindness of others."

Intermarriage has captured the imagination of Americans for more than a century. As Anne Rose shows in her historical study of interfaith families,

Jewish resistance to mixed marriage was often perceived as "tribalism" that contributed to Christian antisemitism. Universalist minister and Tufts College president Elmer Capen warned Jews in the 1890s that they "must violate one of the fundamental regulations" of their "race and take . . . wives from the daughters of the land."[90]

There is no doubt that the propensity of Jewish men—and women—to marry non-Jewish Americans has had exactly the effect that Capen predicted, reinforcing a cycle of toleration. Large numbers of Jews have married non-Jews partially because Jews are so well accepted, and Jews are even more well accepted because so many non-Jewish families include Jewish members. Jewish culture and religious practices have also become familiar, partially because of widespread mixed marriage. Indeed, as we have seen, aspects of Jewish behavior have been adopted by some non-Jews. This familiarity factor has made it easier for Jews in many situations to be strongly culturally identified and/or to adhere to their religious practices. However, despite the comparative ease of Jewish identification and observance, such Jewish connections are limited. Jews with few, if any connections to their Jewish cultural or religious heritages are more numerous than those with intensive connections, and the majority of mixed-married families fall into the weakly-connected category. While mixed marriage makes some Jewish spouses feel more Jewishly identified, it often creates a divided identity in their children. Divided religious identities are problematic from the standpoint of historical definitions of Jewishness. From a sociological standpoint as well, persons with divided religious identities seldom forge strong connections with the Jewish community, culture, or religion.

Every systematic study shows that children are far more likely to grow up identifying as Jews when the whole family feels kinship ties with the Jewish people, and when familial religious experiences—if any—derive from Judaism and no other religion. Inmarriage has been the communal norm for millennia, has played and continues to play a crucial role in creating Jewish social and cultural cohesiveness. However, the often-documented fact that conversionary households have more and deeper Jewish connections than mixed-married households—and than some inmarried households—suggests to many observers that conversion is also a significant strategy for facilitating Jewish cultural transmission, especially in the current environment where numbers of marriages between Jews and non-Jews seem likely to remain high for the foreseeable future.

American Jews face existential issues as they negotiate the first decade of the twenty-first century, and few topics have generated more passionate discussion than intermarriage and its ramifications. When they wrestle with the complicated issues surrounding mixed marriage, individuals, families, communities, leaders and policy planners confront the basic questions "Why be Jewish?" and "What does it mean to be Jewish"?

The answers often depend on who is asking the question, as the diverse voices heard in this book—mixed-married men and women, teenage children of mixed-married families, Jewish communal and religious pronouncements, books, magazines, Internet chat rooms, and other public communications—suggest. For two people in love (and the larger families that care about them), the meaning of a primary relationship may be infinitely more significant than communal concerns. For mixed-married spouses attempting to create meaningful ethnoreligious environments, the needs of their families may be paramount. For American Jewish communities, however, the collective impact of mixed marriage has complex implications grounded in the past and extending into the future.

Scholars, communal and religious leaders frequently reflect on their concerns about the status of spouses, children, and others who are not officially Jewish but think of themselves as "sort of Jewish" or "Jewish and something else" or "might as well be Jewish" (these are all quotes from my study informants). On the left end of the Jewish communal spectrum, some urge that all "fellow travelers" be considered—and computed—as Jews. On the right end of the religious spectrum, some insist that only those who can be certified halakhically be considered as Jews. This issue of status has important personal and societal ramifications, which deserve further, targeted research. Many observers believe that Jewish communities should consider, in the near future, how to come to some type of consensus about this large group of people who are intimately connected to, but not defined as part of the Jewish people, according to current understandings.

Modernity has transformed Jewish options. Nevertheless, many feel that the survivability of Jewishness in any of its definitions depends on Jews who choose to see themselves in thick relationship with Jewish culture and other Jews. The choice to be part of the Jewish people takes place in diverse contexts. Secular Israelis often see themselves in relationship through a political entity, rather than a religious culture. For secular Jews worldwide, the peoplehood link is sometimes experienced through cultural activities and social activism that are perceived as expressions of Jewish values.[91] For Jews who relate to some wing of contemporary Judaism, Jewish peoplehood often has a strong religious aspect.

Each of these groups, despite the differences between their antecedents and beliefs, is profoundly affected by Jewish education. Attachments to Jewish peoplehood and Jewish culture are nurtured and reinforced by informal and formal educational experiences during the teen and adult years, as well as childhood opportunities, as many studies demonstrate. Perhaps most important in light of this book's subject, recent studies show that mixed-married families who seek out Jewish education say they are looking for intellectual and experiential depth, and overwhelmingly prefer substantive, mainstream—rather than popularized—Jewish educational offerings. Thus, inmarried, conversionary, and mixed-married families may each benefit from excellence in educational offerings, and that excellence is one of the few aspects of contemporary life that is directly responsive to Jewish communal efforts.

The potential power of Jewish education, then, may be its ability to create a kind of equality as it opens doors for diverse populations, providing one of the most effective strategies for transmitting knowledge of and attachment to Jewish civilizations and their heritage to the next generation of Jews. By its very nature, the educational enterprise suggests that developing rich connections to Jews and Jewishness is a continuing process for Jews of all sorts, no matter what their status or origins.

Appendix: Tables from the NJPS 2000–2001

Table 1

Married Respondents Inmarried and Intermarried: percentages by parents inmarried and intermarried

		Parental-level intermarriage		
		Inmarried	Intermarried	**Total**
Respondent-level	*Inmarried*	78%	25%	70%
intermarriage	*Intermarried*	22%	75%	30%
Total		100%	100%	100%

Source: Year 2000–2001 National Jewish Population Survey Data (Sylvia Barack Fishman and Ben Phillips, Brandeis University Cohen Center for Modern Jewish Studies). Percentages on all tables are rounded up or down to nearest integer value. Jewish status definitions according to United Jewish Communities. For an overview of the data set, see Mark A. Schulman, "National Jewish Population Survey 2000–2001 Study Review Memo" (unpublished paper, Sept. 2003). A copy of this paper is posted at *www.jewishdatabank.org*. For a summary of findings, see *Strength, Challenge, and Diversity in the American Jewish Population* (*www.ujc.org*, Sept. 2003).

Table 2

*Randomly Selected Child Raised Jewish, Jewish and Some Other Religion,
Jewish Connected, or Not Jewish: percentages by respondents inmarried or
intermarried*

		Respondent-level intermarriage		
		Inmarried	*Intermarried*	**Total**
Jewishness of randomly selected child	Jewish	96%	38%	67%
	Jewish and some other religion, Jewish connected	1%	9%	5%
	Not being raised Jewish	3%	54%	28%
Total		100%	101%	100%

Source: 2000–2001 NJPS data (Sylvia Barack Fishman and Ben Phillips, Brandeis CMJS).
Percentages rounded up or down to the nearest integer value. Jewish status definitions according to UJC.

Table 3

Married Respondents Who Consider Themselves Jewish (By Religion or Secular), Jewish Connected, or Not Jewish: percentages by parents inmarried or intermarried

		Parental-level intermarriage		
		Inmarried	Intermarried	**Total**
Respondent currently	Jewish	91%	29%	72%
Jewish (current religion	Jewish			
Jewish or atheist but	Connected	5%	30%	13%
raised Jewish)	Not Jewish	3%	41%	15%
Total		99%	100%	100%

Source: 2000–2001 NJPS data (Sylvia Barack Fishman and Ben Phillips, Brandeis CMJS). Percentages rounded up or down to the nearest integer value. Jewish status definitions according to UJC.

Table 4

Married Respondents Inmarried and Intermarried: percentages by age

		Age of respondent			
		25–34	35–44	45–54	**Total**
Respondent-level	Inmarried	59%	60%	65%	62%
intermarriage	Intermarried	42%	41%	35%	39%
Total		101%	101%	100%	101%

Source: 2000–2001 NJPS data (Sylvia Barack Fishman and Ben Phillips, CMJS). Percentages rounded up or down to the nearest integer value. Jewish status definitions according to UJC.

Table 5

Married Respondents Inmarried and Intermarried: percentages by gender

		Gender of respondent		Total
		Male	*Female*	
Respondent-level	*Inmarried*	68%	71%	69%
intermarriage	*Intermarried*	33%	29%	31%
Total		101%	100%	100%

Source: 2000–2001 NJPS data (Sylvia Barack Fishman and Ben Phillips, CMJS). Percentages rounded up or down to the nearest integer value. Jewish status definitions according to UJC.

Table 6

Respondents Inmarried and Intermarried: percentages by parents inmarried and intermarried (respondents ages 25–49 and 50 plus)

Age of respondent (split at 50)		Parental-level intermarriage		
		Inmarried	*Intermarried*	*Total*
Age 25–49 **Respondent-level** *intermarriage*	*Inmarried*	72%	21%	60%
	Intermarried	28%	79%	40%
Total		100%	100%	100%
Age 50 + **Respondent-level** *intermarriage*	*Inmarried*	82%	36%	78%
	Intermarried	18%	64%	22%
Total		100%	100%	100%

Source: 2000–2001 NJPS data (Sylvia Barack Fishman and Ben Phillips, CMJS). Percentages rounded up or down to the nearest integer value. Jewish status definitions according to UJC.

Table 7

Randomly Selected Child Being Raised Jewish, Jewish and Some Other Religion,
Jewish Connected, or Not Being Raised Jewish: percentages of inmarried and
intermarried (respondents by ages 25–49 or 50 plus)

Age of respondent (split at 50)		Respondent-level intermarriage		
		Inmarried	*Intermarried*	**Total**
Age 25–49	*Jewish*	97%	39%	69%
Jewishness of randomly selected child	*Jewish and some other religion, Jewish connected*	0%	8%	4%
	Not being raised Jewish	3%	53%	27%
Total		100%	100%	100%
Age 50+	*Jewish*	89%	37%	60%
Jewishness of randomly selected child	*Jewish and some other religion, Jewish connected*	5%	13%	10%
	Not being raised Jewish	7%	50%	31%
Total		101%	100%	101%

Source: 2000–2001 NJPS data (Sylvia Barack Fishman and Ben Phillips, CMJS). Percentages rounded up or down to the nearest integer value. Jewish status definitions according to UJC.

Table 8

Married Respondent Considers Him/Herself Currently Jewish: percentages by
parents inmarried and intermarried (respondents by age 25–49 or 50 plus)

Age of respondent (split at 50)		Parental-level intermarriage		
		Inmarried	*Intermarried*	**Total**
Age 25–49 Respondent currently Jewish (current religion Jewish or atheist but raised Jewish)	*Jewish*	90%	31%	68%
	Jewish connected	5%	29%	14%
	Not Jewish	5%	41%	18%
Total		100%	101%	100%
Age 50+ Respondent currently Jewish (current religion Jewish or atheist but raised Jewish)	*Jewish*	92%	21%	79%
	Jewish connected	6%	25%	9%
	Not Jewish	2%	54%	12%
Total		100%	100%	100%

Source: 2000–2001 NJPS data (Sylvia Barack Fishman and Ben Phillips, CMJS). Percentages rounded up or down to the nearest integer value. Jewish status definitions according to UJC.

Table 9

Married Respondents Inmarried and Intermarried: percentages by gender and ages 25–49 or 50 plus

Age of respondent (split at 50)		Gender of respondent		
		Male	*Female*	**Total**
Age 25–49	*Inmarried*	60%	60%	60%
Respondent-level intermarriage	*Intermarried*	40%	40%	40%
Total		100%	100%	100%
Age 50+	*Inmarried*	73%	80%	77%
Respondent-level intermarriage	*Intermarried*	27%	20%	23%
Total		100%	100%	100%

Source: 2000–2001 NJPS data (Sylvia Barack Fishman and Ben Phillips, CMJS). Percentages rounded up or down to the nearest integer. Jewish status definitions according to UJC.

Notes

Introduction: Following Our Hearts (pp. 1–13)

1. Rebecca Mead, "Comment: Gay Old Times,"*New Yorker* (September 2, 2002): 31–32. Mead is here commenting specifically on the new inclusion of same-sex marriage announcements, but she emphasizes as well that the "religious regulation of marriage has dwindled."

2. Third National Conference of the Dovetail Institute for Interfaith Family Resources, Chicago, 2002. All quotations cited from Dovetail are drawn from the author's fieldnotes on this conference, unless otherwise specified. Dovetail citations will either be attributed anonymously or using pseudonyms to protect the privacy of participants. As further detailed in part III, "Mixed Marriage in Cultural Context," the Dovetail Institute was formed in 1992 to support the ethnoreligious needs of Jewish-Christian interfaith households.

3. Sylvia Barack Fishman, *Jewish and Something Else: A Study of Mixed-Married Families* (New York: American Jewish Committee, 2001) was the initial report on my original research on internal familial dynamics in American Jewish and mixed-married families. We conducted 254 in-depth interviews with husbands and wives in four American locations: New England, New Jersey, Atlanta, and Denver, from 1999 to 2000, augmented by four focus groups with teenagers growing up in mixed-married families. Analysis of these data proceeded through careful reading of the professionally transcribed interviews and through the use of AFTER software. The research was funded by, and *Jewish and Something Else,* which focuses primarily on public policy implications, was published by, the American Jewish Committee in New York. *Double or Nothing?* represents a new and substantially expanded analysis of these and other data.

4. These numbers are rounded from Sergio Della Pergola, "World Jewish Population 2000," in *American Jewish Year Book 2000* (New York: American Jewish Committee, 2000), 484–495.

5. *2000 Annual Survey of American Jewish Opinion* (New York: American Jewish Committee, 2000).

6. Data on children in diverse types of Jewish families according to the 1990 NJPS are from Ariella Keysar, Barry A. Kosmin, and Jeffrey Scheckner, *The Next Generation: Jewish Children and Adolescents* (Albany: State University of New York Press,

2000), 43–58. The Year 2000–2001 National Jewish Population Survey was conducted by the United Jewish Communities (UJC). Data from the 2000–2001 NJPS in this book appear courtesy of the North American Jewish Data Bank at Brandeis University Cohen Center for Modern Jewish Studies.

7. Nathan Glazer and Daniel P. Moynihan, *Beyond the Melting Pot*, 2nd ed. (Cambridge: Massachusetts Institute of Technology Press, 1970); Harold J. Abramson, *Ethnic Diversity in Catholic America* (New York: Whitney Press, 1973); Marcus L. Hansen, "The Third Generation in America," *Commentary* 14 (November 1952): 492–500.

8. Michael Novak, *The Rise of Unmeltable Ethnics: Politics and Culture in the Seventies* (New York: Macmillan, 1973).

9. Gary Tobin and Katherine G. Simon, *Rabbis Talk About Intermarriage* (San Francisco: Institute for Jewish and Community Research, 1999).

10. Jonathan D. Sarna, "The Jews in British America," in Paolo Bernardini and Norman Fiering, eds., *The Jews and the Expansion of Europe to the West, 1450–1800* (New York: Bergahn Books, 2001), 528.

11. Jews arrived to the Hunan province of Central China before 1127 from India or Persia. They built a synagogue, where they stored their sacred scrolls, and became prominent as experts in cotton production and dying, a highly desirable new skill in China, which was suffering from a silk shortage. Although the community maintained aspects of Jewishness for several hundred years, according to the *Encyclopedia Judaica*, "gradually, the Jewish families adopted Chinese customs and surnames. . . . Descendants of some of these families can still be traced locally, but through intermarriage with the Chinese (including Muslims) they more or less lost their Jewish identity." See R. Lowenthal's entry in vol. 10 of the *Encyclopedia Judaica* (Jerusalem), 695–697, which includes a bibliography.

12. Jonathan D. Sarna, personal conversation.

13. Among the articulate voices that have recently set forth this view, see Jack Wertheimer, "Surrendering to Intermarriage," *Commentary* 3, no. 1 (March 2001): 25–32; Bernard Susser and Charles Liebman, *Choosing Survival: Strategies for a Jewish Future* (New York: Oxford University Press, 1999); and Steven Bayme, "The Intermarriage Crisis," in *Jewish Arguments and Counterarguments* (Hoboken, N.J.: Ktav Publishing House, 2002), 223–233.

14. Herbert J. Gans, "Symbolic Ethnicity: The Future of Ethnic Groups and Culture in America," in *Ethnic and Racial Studies* 2 (January 1979): 1–20.

15. Bruce Phillips, *Re-Examining Intermarriage: Trends, Textures & Strategies* (New York: The American Jewish Committee and The Susan and David Wilstein Institute of Jewish Policy Studies, 1993); Rela Mintz Geffen and Egon Mayer, *Intermarrieds in Dialogue* (New York: Center for Jewish Family Life, B'nai B'rith International, and the Jewish Outreach Institute, 1995); Peter Medding, Gary A. Tobin, Sylvia Barack Fishman, and Mordechai Rimor, "Jewish Identity in Conversionary and

Mixed Marriages," *American Jewish Year Book 1992* (New York: American Jewish Committee, 1992), 3–76; Steven M. Cohen, *Religious Stability and Ethnic Decline: Emerging Patterns of Jewish Identity in the United States: A National Survey of American Jews Sponsored by the Florence G. Heller Jewish Community Centers Association Research Center* (Jerusalem: The Hebrew University of Jerusalem Melton Center for Jewish Education in the Diaspora, 1998).

16. Mary C. Waters, *Ethnic Options: Choosing Identities in America* (Berkeley: University of California Press, 1990); Richard Alba, *Ethnic Identity: The Transformation of White America* (New Haven: Yale University Press, 1990).

17. Tamar Jacoby, "An End to Counting by Race?" in *Commentary* 111, no. 6 (June 2001): 37–40, 39.

18. Steven M. Cohen and Arnold M. Eisen, *The Jewish Within: Self, Family and Community in America* (Bloomington: Indiana University Press, 2000), 36. Cohen and Eisen emphasize the importance of "the sovereign self" in religious life journeys, utilizing the term "personalist (to use Liebman's coinage): focused on the self and its fulfillment rather than directed outward to the group."

19. See George G. Iggers, *Historiography in the Twentieth Century: From Scientific Objectivity to the Postmodern Challenge* (Hanover, N.H.: Wesleyan University Press, 1997), 103.

20. Clifford Geertz, "Thick Description: Toward an Interpretive Theory of Culture," in his *Interpretation of Cultures* (New York: Basic Books, 1973).

21. In Iggers, *Historiography*, 123.

22. Geertz, "Thick Description," 5.

23. Eric Hobsbawm, "Inventing Traditions," in *The Invention of Tradition* (Cambridge: Cambridge University Press, 1983), 9.

Part I: Through the Looking Glass (pp. 15–53)

1. In a school or employment setting, social networks are "draped" over the scaffolding of the institutional framework. When one moves from one social circle to another, one moves as well into the new circle's shared ideas, concerns, and values. See Charles Kadushin, "Networks and Circles in the Production of Culture," *American Behavioral Scientist* (1976): 69–84.

2. Waters, *Ethnic Options*, 52–89.

3. Barry A. Kosmin, Egon Mayer, and Ariela Keysar, *American Religious Identification Survey*, 2001 (www.gc.cuny.edu/studies/aris_index.htm); Lawrence R. Iannaccone, "Why Strict Churches Are Strong," *American Journal of Sociology* 99, no. 5 (March 1994): 1180–1211.

4. Mathew Frye Jacobson, in *Whiteness of a Different Color: European Immi-*

grants and the Alchemy of Race (Cambridge: Harvard University Press, 1998), 199, explains that many groups previously perceived to belong to some nonwhite race— such as Jews, Greeks, and Italians—have now been subsumed into a vaguely defined "white" race by many Americans.

5. Recent Gallup polls on trends in U.S. religious beliefs show that Americans are more religious than the populations of many other Western countries. According to a 1995 poll, for example, 96 percent of Americans say they believe in God, compared with 61 percent of British and 70 percent of Canadians. See George Gallup Jr. and Michael Lindsay, *Surveying the Religious Landscape: Trends in U.S. Religion* (Harrisburg, Pa.: 1999), 122.

6. Gans, "Symbolic Ethnicity," 1–20.

7. See Waters, *Ethnic Options, passim.*

8. Paul R. Spickard, *Mixed Blood: Intermarriage and Ethnic Identity in Twentieth-Century America* (Madison: University of Wisconsin Press, 1989), 4.

Part II: Living Mixed Traditions (pp. 55–97)

1. Stephen J. Whitfield, *In Search of American Jewish Culture* (Hanover, N.H.: Brandeis University Press, 1999), 97.

2. Ibid., 99. See his note 27 for Berlin's biographers.

3. Gans, "Symbolic Ethnicity," 1–20.

4. Louis Wirth, *The Ghetto* (Chicago: University of Chicago Press, 1928 and 1956), 240.

5. Glazer and Moynihan, *Ethnicity,* 157–169; Novak, *Unmeltable Ethnics, passim.*

6. Calvin Goldscheider, in *Jewish Continuity and Change: Emerging Patterns in America* (Bloomington: Indiana University Press with the Center for Modern Jewish Studies, Brandeis University, 1986), was the first distinguished sociologist to argue that the American Jewish community had indeed been transformed but was still structurally cohesive.

7. Sylvia Barack Fishman, *Jewish Life and American Culture* (Albany: State University of New York Press, 2000), 15–18.

8. Bernard Lazerwitz, et al., *Jewish Choices: American Jewish Denominationalism* (Albany: State University of New York Press, 1998), gives the most recent statistical analysis of the wings of American Judaism.

9. Sidney Goldstein and Alice Goldstein, *Jews on the Move: Implications for Jewish Identity* (Albany: State University of New York Press, 1996), especially 33–64.

10. Waters, *Ethnic Options,* 122–124.

11. NJPS 2000–2001 data in this book generated by Benjamin Phillips and Sylvia Barack Fishman at CMJS. An overveiw of findings appears in the UJC Report:

Strength, Challenge, and Diversity in the American Jewish Population (www.ujc.org, Sept. 2003).

12. I am grateful to Dr. Charles Kadushin for calling my attention to the relevance of social network theory to my study.

13. Lee F. Gruzen, *Raising Your Jewish/Christian Child: How Interfaith Parents Can Give Their Children the Best of Both Their Heritages* (New York: Newmarket Press, 1990), 218–219.

14. Beth Cousens, "Adult Bat Mitzvah as Entree into Jewish Life for North American Jewish Women" (Waltham, Mass.: Hadassah International Research Institute for Jewish Women at Brandeis University Working Paper, 2002), summarizes recent research and includes original interviews with women who studied for and celebrated adult bat mitzvahs.

15. Moshe Hartman and Harriet Hartman, *Gender Equality and American Jews* (Albany: State University of New York Press, 1996), 227.

16. Linda J. Sax, *America's Jewish Freshmen: Current Characteristics and Recent Trends Among Students Entering College* (Los Angeles: University of California Higher Education Research Institute, Hillel Foundation for Jewish Campus Life, 2002), 54.

17. Developed by such thinkers as Peter Berger and Thomas Luckman in *The Construction of Reality: A Treatise on the Sociology of Knowledge* (Garden City, N.Y.: Anchor Books, 1967) and Malcom Specter and John Kitsuse in *Constructing Social Problems* (New York: Aldine, 1977), the constructionist theory of ethnicity was reevaluated in James A. Holstein and Gale Miller, eds., *Perspectives on Social Problems: Reconsidering Social Constructionism* vol. 5 (New York: Aldine, 1993).

18. Robert N. Bellah, "Competing Visions of the Role of Religion in American Society," in *Uncivil Religion: Religious Hostility in America,* eds. Robert N. Bellah and Frederick E. Greenspahn (New York: Crossroad, 1987), 228.

19. Anthropologist Fredrik Barth is among the more prominent advocates of the view that it is the "ethnic boundary that defines the group, not the cultural stuff it encloses." See *Ethnic Groups and Boundaries: The Social Organization of Cultural Difference* (Boston: Little, Brown, 1969), 15, 17.

20. Joane Nagel, "Constructing Ethnicity: Creating and Recreating Ethnic Identity and Culture," *Social Problems* 41, no. 1 (February 1994): 152–176.

21. John Higham, *Send These to Me: Jews and Other Immigrants in Urban America* (New York: Atheneum, 1975).

22. Alba, *Ethnic Identity,* 199.

Part III: Mixed Marriage in Cultural Contexts (pp. 99–167)

1. Sylvia Barack Fishman, in "Reinventing the Cinematic Jew: Portrayals of Jewish Women and Men in Film," *Report to the Morning Star Commission* (Waltham:

International Research Institute on Jewish Women, Brandeis University, September 1997), reports on the research conducted by the Morning Star Commission in Los Angeles. Members of the Morning Star Commission, created and funded by Hadassah Southern California, chaired by Joan Hyler, and facilitated by Dr. Mara Fein, include film, entertainment, media, and advertising industry executives, artists, writers, and scholars.

Stage one of the Morning Star Commission project created an overview of images of Jewish women and men in film and on television. As part of this overview, I assembled "Reinventing the Cinematic Jew: Portrayals of Jewish Women and Men in Film," a one-hour reel of clips comprised of images of Jews ranging chronologically from films of the late 1920s to contemporary film and television in the 1990s. This reel, prepared under the auspices of the Hadassah International Research Institute for Jewish Women at Brandeis University (HIRIJW), was accompanied by a written discussion of developments in cinematic depiction of Jews.

Stage two of the project explored the impact of media images of Jewish women through focus group research with actual audiences. Claudia Caplan and Barbara Goldberg wrote analyses of the focus group discussions for members of the commission, available as "Jewish Women: The Mirror and the Media" (unpublished manuscript prepared for Hadassah Southern California, The Morning Star Commission, January 1998, Job #1597). These discussions took place on December 7 and 8, 1997, and January 7 and 8, 1998, in communities in and around the Los Angeles area. Some materials in this chapter are adapted from "Picturing Jews and Gender," my analysis of eight focus groups conducted with Jewish and non-Jewish women and men under the auspices of the Morning Star Commission.

2. Michael Alexander, *Jazz Age Jews* (Princeton: Princeton University Press, 2001), 131–179. See also Michael Rogin, *Blackface, White Noise: Jewish Immigrants in the Hollywood Melting Pot* (Berkeley: University of California Press, 1996), and David Zurawik, *The Jews of Prime Time* (Lebanon, N.H.: Brandeis University Press, 2003), a splendid new study released too late to be incorporated into this chapter, especially 78–200, which deal specifically with intermarriage in television plots and characterizations.

3. Sander Gilman, *The Jew's Body* (New York: Routledge, 1991).

4. Jacobson, *Whiteness of a Different Color*, 120.

5. Alexander, *Jazz Age Jews*, 179.

6. Paula Hyman, *Gender and Assimilation in Modern Jewish History: The Roles and Representations of Women* (Seattle: University of Washington Press, 1995), 169.

7. Riv-Ellen Prell, "Rage and Representation: Jewish Gender Stereotypes in American Culture," in Faye Ginsburg and Anna Lowenhaupt Tsing, eds., *Uncertain Terms: Negotiating Gender in American Culture* (Boston: Beacon Press, 1990), 253.

8. In works by prestigious writers such as Philip Wylie and Erik Erikson, Ameri-

can women were derided for dominating and emasculating their husbands and sons. See especially Philip Wylie, *Generation of Vipers* (New York: Holt, Rinehart & Winston, 1942). Some of these issues were first explored in a pioneering book by Charlotte Baum, Paula Hyman, and Sonia Michel, *The Jewish Woman in America* (New York: New American Library, 1978).

9. Jeanine Basinger, *A Woman's View: How Hollywood Spoke to Women, 1930–1960* (Hanover, N.H.: Wesleyan University Press, 1993), 4.

10. Riv-Ellen Prell, "Cinderellas Who (Almost) Never Become Princesses: Subversive Representations of Jewish Women in Postwar Popular Novels," in Joyce Antler, ed., *Talking Back: Images of Jewish Women in American Popular Culture* (Hanover, N.H.: Brandeis University Press, 1998), 127.

11. Philip Roth, *Portnoy's Complaint* (New York: Random House, 1969), 152–153, 146.

12. Laura Mulvey, "Visual Pleasure and Narrative Cinema" (1975), reprinted in Robyn R. Warhol and Diane Price Herndl, eds., *Feminisms: An Anthology of Literary Theory and Criticism* (New Brunswick: Rutgers University Press, 1997), 438–448.

13. See note 1, part III.

14. Gilman, *The Jew's Body*, 174–175.

15. Adrienne Rich, *Blood, Bread and Poetry: Selected Prose 1979–1985* (London: Virago Press, 1986, 110–111.

16. Gilman, *The Jew's Body*, 30, quoting Daphne Merkin, "Dreaming of Hitler," *Esquire* (August 1989): 75–83.

17. Gilman, *The Jew's Body*, 204–205, citing Robert Knox, *The Races of Men* (1850).

18. Philip Roth, *Operation Shylock: A Confession* (New York: Simon & Schuster, 1993), 274–275.

19. *1997 Annual Survey of American Jewish Opinion*, conducted for the American Jewish Committee by Market Facts, Inc. (New York: The American Jewish Committee, 1997).

20. Waters, *Ethnic Options*, 88–89.

21. Bonnie Cousens, email communication to the author, February 18, 2003.

22. Judy Petsonk and Jim Remsen, *The Intermarriage Handbook: A Guide for Jews and Christians* (New York: Arbor House, William Morrow, 1988), 260.

23. Jack Wertheimer, *A People Divided: Judaism in Contemporary America* (Hanover, N.H.: Brandeis University Press, 1993), 101.

24. Gary A. Tobin and Katherine G. Simon, *Rabbis Talk About Intermarriage* (San Franciso: Institute for Jewish & Community Research, 1999), 12.

25. Ellen Jaffee MacClain, *Embracing the Stranger* (New York: Basic Books, 1995).

26. Wertheimer, *A People Divided*, 108.

27. *Intermarried? Reform Judaism Welcomes You* (http://www.uahc.org/outreach/

interfaith.shtml#intro); *Becoming a Jew: Questions and Answers,* in *Outreach and Synagogue Community* (http://uahc.org/outreach/becom.shtml); *Programs and Resources for Interfaith Families and Couples,* in *Outreach and Synagogue Community* (http://uahc.org/outreach/becom.shtml).

28. Daniel M. Klein and Freke Vuijst, *The Half-Jewish Book: A Celebration* (New York: Villard Books, 2000); Petsonk and Remsen, *The Intermarriage Handbook;* Joan C. Hawxhurst, *The Interfaith Family Guidebook: Practical Advice for Jewish and Christian Partners* (Kalamazoo, Mich.: Dovetail Publishing, 1998); Vikki Weiss and Jennifer A. Block, *What To Do When You're Dating a Jew: Everything You Need to Know from Matza Balls to Marriage* (New York: Crown, 2000).

29. David G. Sacks, *Welcoming the Intermarried into Your Jewish Family* (New York: Jewish Outreach Institute, 1995; revised 2000), 4.

30. Ibid.

31. Waters, *Ethnic Options,* 158.

32. Myrna Baron, email announcement of the book launch, entitled "Yossi Beilin Calls for Secular Conversion," 11/17/00. See Yossi Beilin, *His Brother's Keeper: Israel and Diaspora Jewry in the Twenty-First Century* (New York: Schocken Books, 2000).

33. Steven M. Cohen, *Religious Stability and Ethnic Decline: Emerging Patterns of Jewish Identity in the US* (New York: Florence G. Heller/JCC Association Research Center, 1998).

34. Kerry M. Olitzky, "Why We Welcome the Stranger: A Historical Jewish Mandate," in *The State of Jewish Outreach Today: Inaugural Report of the Jewish Outreach Institute* (New York: Jewish Outreach Institute, 2002), 4.

35. Barbara Rosman Penzer, "So You Want to Be a Jewish Mother, but You're Not Jewish," in *The Guide to Jewish Interfaith Family Life,* eds. Ronnie Friedland and Edmund Case (Woodstock: Jewish Lights Publishing, 2001), 98.

36. Shaye Cohen, *The Beginnings of Jewishness: Boundaries, Varieties, Uncertainties* (Berkeley: University of California Press, 1999), 170.

37. Judith Shulevitz, "Bring Back the Sabbath: Why Even the Most Secular Need a Ritualized Day of Rest,"*New York Times Magazine* (March 2, 2003): 50–53.

38. Harvey Cox, *Common Prayers: Faith, Family, and a Christian's Journey Through the Jewish Year* (New York: Houghton Mifflin, 2001).

39. Cohen.

40. Ibid., 261.

41. Albert I. Gordon, *Intermarriage: Interfaith, Interracial, Interethnic* (Boston: Beacon Press, 1964), 89–90.

42. Cox, *Common Prayers,* 143, discussing Rosemary Radford Ruether's *Faith and Fratricide: The Theological Roots of Antisemitism* (New York: Seabury Press, 1974).

43. Bruce Phillips, "Children of Intermarriage: How Jewish?" in *Studies in Contemporary Jewry,* vol. 14 (1998), 81.

44. Fishman, *Jewish Life and American Culture*, 13.

45. Robert N. Bellah, "Competing Visions of the Role of Religion in American Society," in *Uncivil Religion: Interreligious Hostility in America*, eds. Robert N. Bellah and Frederick E. Greenspahn (New York: Crossroad, 1987), 228.

46. Medding, et al., *Year Book*, 15.

47. Ami Eden, "Pollsters Take Off the Gloves in Feud Over Intermarriage," *Forward* (June 15, 2001): 3.

48. Edmund Case, "Discouraging Intermarriage Is Not the Way to Preserve Jewish Identity," *The Jewish Week of New York* (May 18, 2001).

49. Cited by Miriam S. Jerris in "The Silent Minority: Jewish Clergy Who Provide Support for Intermarriage" (Ph.D. dissertation, Union Institute Graduate College, November 2001), 7.

50. Miriam S. Jerris, "Seeing Intercultural Marriages Instead of Interfaith Marriages," on the website <www.shj.org>.

51. Myrna Bonnie Cousens and Ruth Duskin Feldman, eds., *Guide to Humanistic Judaism* (Farmington Hills, Mich.: 1993), 37.

52. Phillips, "Children of Intermarriage," 86.

53. Developed by thinkers such as Peter Berger and Thomas Luckman, in *The Construction of Reality: A Treatise on the Sociology of Knowledge* (Garden City, N.J.: Anchor Books, 1967) and Malcom Spector and John Kitsuse, in *Constructing Social Problems* (New York: Aldine, 1977), the constructionist theory of ethnicity was reevaluated in James A. Holstein and Gale Miller, eds., *Perspectives on Social Problems: Reconsidering Social Constructionism* (New York: Aldine, 1993).

54. Anthropologist Frederik Barth is among the more prominent advocates of the view that it is the "ethnic boundary that defines the group, not the cultural stuff that it encloses," in *Ethnic Groups and Boundaries: The Social Organization of Cultural Difference* (Boston: Little, Brown, 1969), 15, 17.

55. Joane Nagel, "Constructive Ethnicity: Creating and Recreating Ethnic Identity and Culture," *Social Problems* 41, no. 1 (February 1994): 153.

56. One example of those who view the nuclei as the definers of ethnic distinctiveness is John Higham; see *Send These to Me: Jews and Other Immigrants in Urban America* (New York: Atheneum, 1975).

57. Wexner Fellowship Summer Institute Plenary Lecture, Vermont, 2001.

58. Steven Bayme, director of the William Petschek National Jewish Family Center of the American Jewish Committee, wrote the following in his introduction to *Jewish and Something Else* "The rise of dual-faith homes, practicing a mixture of Judaism and Christianity, brings religious syncretism that undermines the integrity of both faiths. The nature of Jewish identification in such homes is being so radically redefined as to become unrecognizable, forfeiting distinctive Judaic ethos—to say nothing of Jewish continuity. . . . In the face of an American culture that has declared

interfaith marriage to be as American as apple pie, only Jews themselves can articulate the importance of Jewish inmarriage. The question is whether Jewish leaders have the will to do so" (v–vi).

59. Jack Wertheimer, "Surrendering to Intermarriage," in *Commentary* 111, no. 3 (March 2001); 32.

60. *The State of Jewish Outreach Today: Inaugural Report of the Jewish Outreach Institute,* New York (November 2002), 16.

61. Malcom Gladwell, *The Tipping Point: How Little Things Can Make a Big Difference* (New York: Little, Brown, 2000).

62. Fern Chertok, Mark Rosen, Amy Sales, and Len Saxe, *Outreach Families in the Sacred Common: Congregational Responses to Interfaith Issues* (Waltham, Mass.: Cohen Center for Modern Jewish Studies at Brandeis University, sponsored by UAHC-CCAR Commission on Reform Jewish Outreach, 2001), 16.

63. Ibid., 14–15.

64. Ibid., 24–25.

65. Political opinion surveys and exit polls continue to show American Jews to be an overwhelmingly liberal population. Conservative political and social attitudes are more likely to be found among the following American Jewish subgroups: the fervently Orthodox, Jews living in some deep South locations (but not Miami), ideological Neo-Conservatives, and a limited proportion of very wealthy Jews, most of whom continue to exhibit liberal tendencies.

66. Chester E. Finn Jr., "Teachers, Terrorists, and Tolerance," in *Commentary* 112, no. 5 (December 2001): 54.

67. Randy Cohen, "The Ethicist: Group Dating," *New York Times Magazine* (October 14, 2001): 40.

68. Aliza Phillips, "The Hora: Gentiles Are Taking Hold of a Jewish Wedding Tradition," *Forward* (November 22, 2001): 1.

69. See Charles Kadushin, *Introduction to Social Network Theory,* (forthcoming), 32–33. Kadushin here draws primarily on the work of Nan Lin, "Building a Network Theory of Social Capital," in *Connections* (1999).

70. Rebecca Meade, "Department of Commitment: Unmarital Bliss," *New Yorker* (December 9, 2002): 58, 50.

71. Ellen O'Brien, "Oy, My (Pseudo) Jewish Mother," in *Boston Globe Magazine* (February 23, 2003): 5.

72. See Gish Jen, *Mona in the Promised Land* (New York: Vintage Books, 1997); the phrase is taken from the title of her previous novel, *Typical American* (Boston: Houghton Mifflin, 1991).

73. Philip Roth, *The Human Stain* (Boston: Houghton Mifflin, 2000).

74. Robert Wuthnow, *Growing Up Religious: Christians and Jews and Their Journeys of Faith* (Boston: Beacon Press, 1999), 12–13.

75. Wuthnow, *Growing Up Religious,* 51.

76. Sarna, "Jews in British America," 528.

77. Phillips, "Children of Mixed Marriage," 91–92.

78. Alan Dershowitz, *The Vanishing American Jew: In Search of Jewish Identity for the Next Century* (New York: Little, Brown, 1997), 298–300.

79. Wuthnow, *Growing Up Religious,* xxxvii, quoting Madeline L'Engle, *The Irrational Season* (New York: Seabury Press, 1979), 16–17.

80. Wuthnow, *Growing Up Religious,* xxxvii; Iannaccone, "Strict Churches."

81. Alba, *Jewish Life in American Culture.*

82. Chertok, et. al., *Outreach Families,* 10.

83. Cox, *Common Prayers,* 250–251.

84. See Tamar Jacoby, "An End to Counting by Race?" in *Commentary* 111, no. 6 (June 2001): 37–40.

85. Jonathan D. Sarna, *A New History of American Judaism* (New Haven: Yale University Press, forthcoming).

86. Gabrielle Glaser, *Strangers to the Tribe: Portraits of Interfaith Marriage* (Boston: Houghton Mifflin, 1997), 197.

87. R. A. Schermerhorn, *Comparative Ethnic Relations* (Chicago: University of Chicago Press, 1970, 1978), as cited by Werner Sollors, *Theories of Ethnicity: A Classical Reader* (New York: New York University Press, 1996), xii.

88. Michael Walzer, "The Present of the Past," reviewing Avishai Margalit, *The Ethics of Memory* (Cambridge: Harvard University Press, 2002), in *The New Republic* 228, no. 4 (January 20, 2003): 36–37.

89. Jacqueline Savaiano, "Quyen Nguyen and Benjamin Loeb," *New York Times Weddings/Celebrations* (Sunday, March 16, 2003): 11.

90. Peter J. Thuesen, "Children of the Religious Enlightenment: The Question of Interfaith Marriage in Nineteenth-Century America," in *Reviews in American History* 31 (2003): 39–46, 43, quoting from Anne C. Rose, *Beloved Strangers: Interfaith Families in Nineteenth-Century America* (Cambridge: Harvard University Press, 2001), 122.

91. The *Guide to Humanistic Judaism* states that "Humanistic Judaism is a nontheistic alternative in contemporary Jewish life. It was established by Rabbi Sherwin T. Wine in 1963 in Detroit, Michigan." The guide lists a number of humanistic Jewish affirmative principles and includes an alphabetical series of definitions from Adoption and Adult Ceremonies to Yizkor and Youth Education, along with the organization's mission statement and a list of resources and publications.

Index

Abie's Irish Rose, 102
Abramson, Harold J., 178n7
African Americans, 103, 108, 156
Alba, Richard, 10, 96, 161, 179n16
Alexander, Michael, 182n2
Allen, Woody, 45, 106–8
ambivalence, 32–33, 84, 86, 94, 95, 157
American culture: coalescence in, 131,
    132, 154, 158; cultural resistance and
    community formation, 160–61;
    decline of Jewish identity, 8–9, 103;
    in film, 102–3, 105, 107–9, 117, 154;
    inclusivity and, 132, 150; interfaith
    romance, 2, 21–24, 102–3, 106; Jew-
    ish men and, 102–4, 106–7; Judaiza-
    tion of, 154–56; multiculturalism and,
    4–6, 42–43, 48–50; passing, 28,
    85–86, 110, 121–22; race in, 103,
    106–10, 112, 152–54, 156, 161–62;
    religious identity in, 48–49, 180n4; on
    religious syncretism, 95, 96, 122, 156;
    in television, 110–12, 116, 118–19,
    122, 156; whiteness, 103, 106–7, 156;
    women and, 103–4, 106–7. *See also*
    assimilation; Christianity; mixed
    marriage
American Jewish Committee, xv, 6, 115,
    177n3, 177n5
American Religious Identification Survey
    2001 (ARIS), 44–45
Annie Hall, 107, 108
*Annual Survey of American Jewish Public
    Opinion* (1997), 115
antisemitism: assimilation and, 3, 22–23;
    in childhood environment, 28, 120–21;
    in film, 104, 107, 108, 109; "Jewing
    him down," use of, 113, 114, 121;
    Jewish American princess in, 22, 105;
    Jewish men and, 113–14, 117; socio-
    economic upward mobility, 117. *See*

also materialism; race and racism;
    stereotypes, Jewish
Antler, Joyce, 183n10
assimilation: antisemitism, 3, 22–23; con-
    version, 3, 133–35, 136; Emancipation,
    3, 135–36; ethnicity, 3, 57–58; *The
    Jazz Singer* and, 102–3; materialism
    and, 22–23; mixed marriage and, 143;
    pluralism, 9. *See also* Christmas obser-
    vances; converts/conversionary fami-
    lies; Jewish identity
As Told by Ginger, 122, 123, 156
atheism, 136–37

bar/bat mitzvah ceremonies, 80, 82–83,
    93, 142, 144, 181n14
Baron, Myrna, 184n32
Barth, Fredrik, 181n19, 185n54
Basinger, Jeanine, 105, 183n9
Baum, Charlotte, 182n8
Bayme, Steven, 146, 147, 178n13,
    185n58
Beilin, Yossi, 130, 184n32
Bellah, Robert N., 96, 138–39, 181n18,
    185n45
Berger, Peter, 181n17
Berlin, Irving, 57
birth ceremonies, 77–81, 93
birthright israel program, 149
blended families, 74
Block, Jennifer, 184n28
brit milah (ritual circumcision), 77–81,
    85, 93

Caplan, Claudia, 181n1
Case, Edmund, 141, 184n35, 185n48
Catholicism, 29, 30, 37, 45, 52, 53, 59
ceremonies: baptism, 71, 77; bar/bat mitz-
    vah, 80, 82–83, 93, 142, 144, 181n14;
    brit milah (ritual circumcision), 77–81,

ceremonies (*continued*):
85, 93; cohabitation ceremony (Com-mitzvah), 155; coming of age, inter-faith, 83; Shalom Bat, 93; weddings, 1, 40–44, 48, 126–27, 154, 177n1

Chertok, Fern, 186n62

children in mixed-married households: bar/bat mitzvah ceremonies, 82–83, 84, 142, 181n14; Christmas obser-vances, 62, 63, 68; church education of, 129; college students as, 68, 88; Jewish identity of, 6–7, 94–95, 143, 170t2, 174t7, 175t8; marriage patterns of, 6–7, 31–32, 169t1, 172t5, 173t6; mothers and, 86, 87, 88; New Testa-ment readings with, 63, 139–40; pre-marital discussions of childrearing, 50, 51–52, 72; return inmarriage of, 159–60; ritual circumcision (*brit milah*) of, 77–81, 85, 93; teenagers, 18–20, 27–28, 60, 70, 83–84, 90, 94–95, 157–58. *See also* ceremonies; inmarriage; intermarriage; Jewish identity; Jewish observances

children raised as Jews: age of parents and, 7, 175t8; Christmas observances and, 68; church attendance of, 67, 74; cultural continuity and, 31–35, 91, 160–61; influence of extended family on, 65–66, 69, 70, 72–73, 81–82, 158; interfaith advocacy institutions on, 141; marriage patterns of, 169t1, 170t2; synagogue attendance of, 69. *See also* ceremonies; inmarriage; intermarriage; Jewish identity; Jewish observances

Christianity: Catholicism, 29, 30, 37, 45, 52, 53, 59; church attendance, 67, 74; conversion to, 3, 136; as cultural, 62, 63, 68; importance to non-Jewish spouses, 2, 52, 89–90; in interfaith households, 74, 94–95; Jewish out-marriers on, 32–33; on Judaism, 52, 96, 136; New Testament and, 63, 139–40; Pentacostalism, 45. *See also* converts/conversionary families; Jewish identity; mixed marriage

Christmas observances: Christmas trees, 61, 64–65, 68, 75, 145; conversionary

families and, 66, 96; as cultural enrich-ment, 62, 63, 68; December dilemma, 60, 64, 149; in dual-faith families, 61–62; gift giving and, 66–67; Hanukkah observances and, 60, 61–62, 65–66; household religious identity defined by, 60; inmarriages and, 68, 96; as Jewish identity bound-ary, 96; Jewish spouses assisting with, 74; mothers and, 73, 86; parents of mixed-married couples and, 65–68, 69, 72–73, 81–82

circumcision, 77–81, 85, 93

coalescence, 131, 132, 154, 158

Cohen Center for Modern Jewish Studies (Brandeis University), 148–49, 161, 169t1, 170t2, 171t3–4, 172t5, 173t6, 174t7, 175t8, 176t9, 177n6, 180n11

Cohen, Randy, 153–54, 161, 186n67

Cohen, Shaye, 132–34, 184n36

Cohen, Steven M., 10, 131, 178n15, 179n18, 184n33

Conservative Judaism, 143–46

converts/conversionary families: children of, 38, 67; Christmas observances of, 66, 96; family attitudes towards, 37, 66–67; history of conversion, 3, 133–35, 136; Jewish education and, 31, 167; Jewish identity of, 144–45, 157, 165; patrilineal descent and, 127–28; religious observance negoti-ated in, 91; secular conversion in Israel, 130–31; support for, 70– 71, 148–49; synagogues and, 69, 148

Cousens, Beth, 181n14

Cousens, Bonnie (Myrna Bonnie), 125, 185n51

Cox, Harvey, 133, 162, 184n38

dating: choice in, 23, 29, 119; household religion discussed while, 50, 51–52, 72; Internet dating, 153–54, 155; parental guidance on, 34–36; romance, inter-faith and, 2, 21–24, 102–3, 106. *See also* inmarriage; intermarriage

December dilemma, 60, 64, 149

Della Pergola, Sergio, 177n4

Dershowitz, Alan, 160, 187n78

inmarriage (*continued*):

Jewish identity in, 144–45, 170t2, 172t5; Jewish identity of adult children, 143, 171t3; parents' encouragement of, 35–36; religious observance negotiated in, 91; return inmarriage and, 159–60; synagogue attendance and, 69

InterfaithFamily.com, 141

intermarriage. *See* mixed marriage

Israel, State of, 3, 28–29, 130–31, 149, 164

Jacobson, Matthew Frye, 179n4, 182n4

Jacoby, Tamar, 179n17, 187n84

The Jazz Singer, 102–3

Jen, Gish, 156, 186n72

Jerris, Miriam S., 185n49, 185n50

Jewish education: bar/bat mitzvah ceremonies and, 80, 93; blended families and, 74; conversionary families and, 31, 167; dual-faith families and, 140; Hebrew school attendance, 80, 81; impact on childrearing, 31; inmarriage and, 27, 31, 159, 167; Jewish literacy, 88, 157, 160, 161; Jewish spouses on, 81–82, 85, 87, 95; in outreach programs, 161; return inmarriage and, 160. *See also* Jewish identity

Jewish identity: of adult children of mixed-marriage households, 7, 143, 171t3, 175t8; African Americans and, 103, 108, 156; bar/bat mitzvah ceremonies and, 82–83, 93, 142, 181n14; in blended families, 74; chauvinism, 149–50; of children, 7, 52–53, 67, 78–79, 94–95, 128, 143, 170t2, 174t7, 175t8; coalescence and, 131, 132, 154, 158; of college students, 68, 88; of conversionary families, 144–45, 157, 165; decline of, 8–9, 103; as different, 28, 49, 96, 120, 139; in dual-faith families, 83; friendship circles in, 18, 24, 27, 159, 179n1; inclusivity and, 132–35, 150–51; of inmarried families, 144–45, 172t5; Israel and, 28–29, 130–31, 149; Jews in Christian families and, 122–23; liberalism in, 24–25, 115, 149–50, 186n65; mothers and, 85,

86, 88, 102, 105, 128; of NJPS respondents, 7, 171t3, 171t4, 175t8; not being Christian as, 139; passing as non-Jewish, 28, 121–22; patrilineal descent and, 127–28, 134–35; self-perceptions of, 112–13, 115–16; social networks, 71–72, 85, 92–93, 128–29, 154, 164. *See also children headings;* Christmas observances; inmarriage; intermarriage; stereotypes, Jewish

Jewish observances: Hanukkah, 60, 61–62, 65–66; kashruth, 89, 91, 133; Passover, 32, 61–64, 69, 73, 75, 86; Rosh Hashanah, 62; Sabbath, 70, 133; synagogue attendance, 69; teenagers, 28, 90, 95; Yom Kippur, 62

Jewish Outreach Institute (JOI), 129–30, 131–32, 147

Jewish society, historical, 3, 132–35, 136, 158–59, 163–64

Judaism: Christianity on, 52, 96, 136; Conservative, 143–46; Humanistic, 125, 142–43, 187n91; Jewish spouses on, 32–33, 53–54, 70, 87, 90–91; non-Jewish spouses on, 75, 82, 88–91, 157, 162; Orthodox, 31, 38, 143, 144; Reconstructionist, 127; Reform, 124–29, 145, 161

Kadushin, Charles, 179n1, 180n12, 186n69

Keysar, Ariella, 177n6, 179n3

Kitsuse, John, 181n17

Klein, Daniel M., 184n28

Kosmin, Barry A., 177n6, 179n3

Lazerwitz, Bernard, 180n8

Lieberman, Joseph, 5

Liebman, Charles, 146, 147, 178n13, 179n18

Lin, Nan, 186n69

Lindsay, Michael, 180n5

Luckman, Thomas, 181n17

MacClain, Ellen Jaffee, 183n25

Margalit, Avishai, 163, 187n88

materialism: assimilation and, 22–23; "Jewing him down," use of, 113; Jew-

Scheckner, Jeffrey, 177n6
Schermerhorn, R. A., 187n87
Schulman, Mark A. (SRBI), 10, 169t1
secular Jewish humanist movement, 125, 142–43, 187n91
Shrage, Barry, 146
Shulevitz, Judith, 133, 184n37
Simon, Katherine G., 178n9, 183n24
social networks, 71–72, 85, 92–93, 128–29, 154, 164
Sollors, Werner, 187n87
Specter, Malcolm, 181n17
Spickard, Paul R., 180n8
spouses, Jewish: on bar/bat mitzvah ceremonies, 82; children of, 50, 51–53, 62–63, 78–79, 87; on Christian holiday observances, 28, 61, 62, 64–65, 67–68, 73–74; on conversion, 90; desirability of, 119, 155; fairness, 61, 73, 74, 157; identification boundaries for non-Jewish spouses, 53–54; Jewish education of, 78, 81–82; Jewish involvement expected by non-Jewish spouses, 50, 70, 72, 82; on Judaism, 32–33, 53–54, 70, 87, 90–91; on ritual circumcision (brit milah), 77–81, 85, 93
spouses, non-Jewish: conversion of, 87, 92, 128, 129, 148–49; explaining Christian roots to Jewish-raised children, 91; Hebrew language acquisition, 88, 157; home background of, 18–19; identification boundaries for Jewish spouses, 53–54; on Jewish children and Christian observances, 62–63, 86; on Jewish involvement of Jewish partner, 50, 70, 72, 82; on Judaism, 69, 75, 82, 88–91, 157, 162; on Passover seder, 63–64; on ritual circumcision (brit milah), 77–81, 85, 93; secularism, 160
stereotypes, Jewish: as domineering, 109–10, 116; in films, 102–3, 105, 107–9, 117, 154; intellectualism and, 24–25; Jewish American princess, 22, 105, 126; of Jewish women, 104, 108–11, 116, 118, 182n8; of men, 29, 108; as money-hoarding, 113–15; as neurotic, 23, 107; physical appearance, 109–11, 117–18; real-life perceptions

of Jews, 109; return inmarriage, 160; secularism, 8, 124–25, 142–43, 187n91; self-denigration and, 113–15; upward mobility, 106–7, 117; voice as, 109, 111–12
Strength, Challenge and Diversity in the American Jewish Population (UJC), 169t1, 180n11
Susser, Bernard, 178n13
synagogues, 69, 71, 89, 127, 148

teenagers: bar/bat mitzvah ceremonies and, 80, 82–83, 93, 142, 144, 181n14; extended family's influence on, 19–20, 70, 157–58; friendship circles, 27; on interfaith upbringing, 83, 94–95; Jewish identity of, 27, 28, 83–84, 90, 91, 95; parents' ambivalence about religious commitments, 91, 94; religion, attitudes towards, 18, 60
television: *As Told by Ginger*, 122, 156; Jewish women in, 110, 111, 112, 116, 118–19; religious syncretism in, 122, 156; *Thirtysomething*, 122, 156
Thuesen, Peter J., 187n90
Tobin, Gary A., 178nn9, 15, 183n24
Tsing, Anna Lowenhaupt, 182n7

United Jewish Communities (UJC), 7, 169t1, 170t2, 171t3, 4, 172t5, 173t6, 174t7, 175t8, 176t9, 178n6

Vuijst, Freke, 184n28

Walzer, Michael, 163, 187n88
Warhol, Robyn R., 183n12
Waters, Mary, 10, 30, 50, 59, 120, 130, 179n16
Weddings: announcements, 1, 177n1; civil ceremonies, 43, 44; cohabitation ceremony (Commitzvah), 155; Jewish rituals in, 40–41, 154; multiple religious rituals in, 42–43, 48; rabbis and Christian clergy as co-officiants, 126–27; separate ceremonies in two religions, 42–43
Weiss, Vikki, 184n28
Wertheimer, Jack, 146–47, 178n13, 183n23

whiteness, 103, 106–7, 108, 156
Whitfield, Stephen J., 180n1
Wine, Sherwin, 187n91
Wirth, Lewis, 57, 180n4
women, Jewish: body image of, 110–11, 118; as domineering, 108–10, 116; family and, 104–5, 116–17; incidence of mixed marriage, 7, 172t5; Jewish American princess, 22, 105, 126; Jewish men and, 20–21, 103–4, 108–9, 111, 119; materialism of, 116, 117–18; media images of, 103, 110, 111, 112, 116, 118–19; passing as non-Jewish, 121–22; socioeconomic mobility, 117; voice of, 109, 111–12

women, non-Jewish: as American culture, 103–4, 106–7; conversion, 128; as escape from Jewish family, 5, 20–21, 106; individualism and, 20–21, 108–9; on Jewish women's behavior, 116; physical attractiveness of, 117–18
Woody Allen, 45, 106–8
Wuthnow, Robert, 156, 158, 160, 186n74
Wylie, Philip, 182n8

Yom Kippur, 75

Zurawik, David, 182n2